# Start Computing Here

## By

## Anthony Saulnier

# *Start Computing Here*

ISBN# 978-1-4357-0290-5

Published by lulu.com

# About The Author

Anthony is a *Microsoft* and *Comptia* certified professional who graduated from Seneca College in Toronto, Ontario.

He was born and raised in Yarmouth, Nova Scotia, Canada and moved to Toronto in 2000 to embark on a career in information technology. While living in Yarmouth, he served close to 7 years as a volunteer firefighter with the *Yarmouth Fire Department*, and worked in his family's restaurant business for over 5 years before deciding to get into the information technology industry.

Having taken technology training from both *Humber and Seneca Colleges*, he graduated from *Seneca* in March of 2004. The same week he graduated, he started his own computer repair business for home users.

In addition to operating his own computer repair business, he has worked in technical roles for *Microsoft* internal vendors, *Seneca College*, the *Canadian Diabetes Association*, and *Thindesk Inc*.

After starting work in the information technology industry, Anthony realized that there was a need for non-technical professionals to be educated. He noticed that more often than not, ordinary people were being misled, sometimes intentionally, sometimes unintentionally. This is what prompted him to start writing his book.

Anthony plans to write follow-up editions for both home users and businesses as technology changes. Be sure to check new editions as they come out.

# *Table of Contents*

**CHAPTER**

# Introduction

My name is Anthony Saulnier. I am an experienced computer technician and I currently operate my own home based computer and information technology service out of the Toronto area servicing home and small business computer users. I also work for major businesses providing information technology related services, namely troubleshooting and repairing computers and servers. In the past, I have provided technical services for *Microsoft*, *Seneca College*, the *Canadian Diabetes Association*, and *Thindesk Inc*, which is based out of the Greater Toronto Area. Thindesk Inc is a service provider that provides remotely managed services for small to medium sized businesses that are unable to hire full time technical staff.

There are many situations that I run into where problems could have been avoided if the customer had known ahead of time what issues could arise as the result of certain actions and if they had a good understanding of technology. Sometimes customers are unsure of where to turn to initially for assistance, or how to troubleshoot basic computer problems, or, they just do not know what technology to look for when they are looking to make a purchase of any type.

My life experiences and observance of the lack of education material such as this have prompted me to write this book. Let's face it, when you go to a bookstore and look at the computer book section, most books assume that you already have a working computer and computer knowledge.

Every day, I see the good, the bad, and the ugly in information technology. I have seen everything from systems working properly for long periods-of-time, to dishonest people and businesses, to customers who make unwise choices. Some people tend to go with the cheapest solution they can find for anything they purchase, but when it comes to computer technology, the cheapest solution can become the most expensive solution.

My plan is to follow up on this book with subsequent versions as technology changes and new computer operating systems are released. Specifically, I plan to include information about *Microsoft's Vista* operating system in my next release. I do also plan to write a book for small to medium sized businesses that require information technology expertise, but cannot afford to purchase their own equipment and hire full time technical staff.
For the most part, I do not give quoted or estimated prices simply because the prices for software and components change on a daily basis, but any prices quoted or estimated in my book are in Canadian dollars, and are based on 2007 average prices.

Should you have any questions, you can contact me by email at
anthonysaulnier@anthonysaulnier.com

# Why This Book is for You!

This book is one of the most important technology related books that you will read, especially if you are an inexperienced technology user, so I highly recommend that you read it carefully. While I did try my best to not be overly technical, the technical information that I have written in this book is handy for you to understand, so I have explained things to you. In addition, what I have done is place a terminology and picture section at the end of the book for your general reference.

How many times do you go into a bookstore to look for a computer book to help you with your new or first computer purchase? How many books out there give you tips on how to get good quality and service? Sadly, few books like mine help people who are not technical professionals in the way that I will help you.

This book is not designed to teach you how to use a computer, however, it is designed to give you many great tips to make your computing experience greater. It is more or less a buyers guide, but with no advertisements, just good advice

Ask yourself, when is the last time you bought something for your computer, and never bothered to get any professional opinions? I see people do these things day in and day out, and I just think to myself, are these people not using their heads? Are they stubborn? Do they know it all? When something goes wrong though, they get upset and take it out on other people. Seeing this prompted me to start writing this book.

Perhaps you are interested in purchasing a new computer or laptop, or a piece of hardware or software and you are not sure what you should purchase and where to purchase it from. Perhaps you need some advice about getting service and technical support. Maybe you want to learn about security or maybe you want get familiar with computers and get ideas in different areas of computing. Maybe you are having technical difficulties and you have no idea where or who to turn to.

I have designed this book mainly for home and small to medium size business users who are of the non-technical type. It will provide you with an outstanding level of knowledge regarding the purchasing of computers, peripherals, software, and services. Specifically, you will learn what is required to operate your computer. You will learn what traits to look for in terms of good and bad quality and service, and many of the common technologies available. I will even give you ideas on where to obtain assistance and training programs, tips on how to secure your computer or small network, ideas on how to backup your data, and last but never really least, tips on how to troubleshoot some common computer problems. I also give you some insight on non-ethical business practices that have a major effect on you, the customer, and how to avoid the types of people and businesses that are un-ethical.

Frankly, most people will be surprised about some of the things that do not come to their minds when purchasing and making important technology related decisions. After all, we are human and cannot think of everything all the time. We also make mistakes sometimes. I hope that I will stop you from making a big mistake in the future.

You will be making a wise decision by reading my book. My book goes straight-to-the-point without most of the gibberish seen in other books. I also provide good examples from my personal experience.

# How To Read This Book

➤ Represents an important point that you absolutely need to know.

❖ Represents a story that I have to tell.

● Represents an important piece of advice or a good tip.

\* Represents an item that is described or explained in the terminology section at the end of the book. These items are described in detail in the general section of the book

# Understanding the Basics Before Buying

Understanding the basics is an integral part to purchasing, understanding, and using computer products and services. My book will help you in ways that you never thought were possible. If you are the type of person that thinks you know everything there is to know about computers, then you might want to reconsider a few things because even the most knowledgeable I.T. person does not know everything there is to know about every component and software package. With that said, I want to make sure that you have a good understanding of the concepts, especially the basics.

Remember, technology changes, but most concepts do not. Understanding the concepts will help you a great deal.

## Why The Price Difference?

First, I highly recommend that you invest your money wisely by purchasing your components and software from somewhere reputable, where you are sure that you will not be purchasing damaged or refurbished equipment, or rogue software for that matter.

If a computer costs $1500 at store A and that exact same computer costs $1000 at store B, then you should tread very lightly; do not assume you are being ripped off by store A, it's possible store B is selling bad or skimmed down equipment. Cheaper is not always better, especially if you are always replacing something. Perhaps both computers are of a good quality, but more comes with purchasing the computer at store A.

I have seen too many cases where the cheap road ends up becoming the most expensive road, all because some people do not invest wisely the first time around. Why bother purchasing cheaper items if you always have to replace them? In the end, you end up paying more money and you end up with more headaches. Also, consider the environment. If you purchase something of high quality, it will last longer so you will have to replace it less often. This will mean a lower number of products being produced, thus reducing the amount of materials used and harm done to the environment.

> Read all of the purchasing tips that I have suggested in this book; I promise they will be worth reading.

**STOP – READ BEFORE YOU BUY:**

**(1)** Inquire about warranties. For more information, see the *warranties* section in this book. Maybe you do not get a good warranty plan with the cheaper item.

**(2)** Find out what components and software come with the items that you are interested in purchasing. You may get more value for your money with the more expensive item.

**(3)** Check the items for physical damage, scratches, and dents because the cheaper item may be damaged.

**(4)** Check the reputation of the store. If the service is terrible, chances are the component quality is terrible as well. You may end up paying more in the end due to poor quality items that consistently need replacing.

**(5)** Find out what type of support is available. Is there a toll free number? Is email support the only option available? The problem with email support is that it can sometimes take a few days to resolve certain issues. On the other hand, its advantage is that you can save the email responses for future reference.

**(6)** Be wary of advertisements. If a store is advertising bundles of free software for new computers, there may be catches that they are not telling you about (e.g. mandatory contracts or software expiry after 60 days). Even worse, they may be able to afford to give you the extras because they are using extremely cheap quality hardware. Remember, you do not usually get something for free.

**(7)** Read my section called *Shopping for Software, Hardware, & Services*. I will provide you with some tips that most people do not even think about.

You will also need to take into consideration how much money you can afford to spend, and what you want to do with the computer system. If you like playing high-end graphic games or if you want a good media center computer, then you are going to need to spend a fair amount of money on hardware and software. At the current time of writing, it is common for people to have to spend $1400 or more for a computer system to play high end games or to use as a media center.

If you are only going to be doing some word processing work, email, Internet chat, or running programs that are not graphic intensive, then you do not have to purchase or build a true gaming system.

Always listen to your instincts. If you are like me, your gut feeling is usually right. If you have a feeling that a sales person is not being truthful, or that a product may be bad, then leave. If needed, seek the help of a non-biased qualified person who has no interest in what brand you purchase or where you purchase it.

- A biased person with an interest might be someone who represents the product manufacturer, store, or a salesperson on commission.

➢ Also, CHECK YOUR ITEMS FOR DAMAGE OR MISSING PARTS BEFORE PURCHASING THEM.

Now, let's talk briefly about the basic components and software for your computer.

**The Absolute Requirements Needed To Operate Your Computer:**

The most basic requirements are:

➢ The video card[1]
➢ Motherboard[2]
➢ Memory
➢ CPU (central processing unit, or processor)
➢ Motherboard case
➢ Power supply
➢ Keyboard
➢ Mouse
➢ Monitor
➢ CD-Rom,
➢ Hard drive
➢ Operating System Software

If you are missing one of these components, you will have a hard time using your computer, and it may not function at all.

---

[1] The video card is the hardware device that enables you to connect your computer monitor to your computer. Video cards are either integrated directly onto the motherboard, or they are added as an additional card that fits into either a *PCI* slot or a special accelerated graphics port on the motherboard, also known as an *AGP* slot.
[2] The motherboard is the largest circuit board inside a computer. It connects all of your computer hardware together and has various slots for the CPU, drives, memory, and additional hardware devices.

For a pre-built computer system (not a complete system with a monitor, keyboard, and mouse), your computer case will contain the motherboard, power supply, CPU, CD/DVD-ROM (or a similar device), memory, and a hard drive. These are all are required for your computer to operate. You will also need to purchase an operating system as well, if it is not pre-installed for you.

- When purchasing a new computer (not a used or refurbished computer), ask about getting a recovery CD. These things are great to have, and are necessary if you need to re-install your computers operating system. I would be wary of any brand new brand name computer system that does not come with this CD.

- Recovery CDs often format and remove all files and software from a computer when you use these CDs, therefore back up your important files and hardware device drivers before using these CDs. You should get in the habit of backing up your important files on a regular basis anyway.

- You should also ask for a driver CD. This contains the software required to allow your computer to communicate with the hardware that came with it. The driver software may or may not already be included on the recovery CD. The most important driver software that you will most likely have to install is for your network card, which is instrumental in providing you with an Internet connection. Once you have an Internet connection, you can often download other driver software for the remaining components from each of the manufacturer's web sites.

  If you purchase new hardware after you purchase your computer, the new hardware should come with its own driver disk. Some exceptions to this rule include ATA hard drives, RAM, and USB external drives.

- Also, ask the salesperson what other components come with the computer system. Do not expect to receive peripherals such as printers, scanners, or all-in-one devices at no additional cost. However, you should expect to receive a monitor, keyboard, mouse, and small set of speakers if you are purchasing a "full system".

## Motherboards:

The motherboard is the main circuit board inside your computer that brings everything together. It is the device that connects all of your components together. With that said, it is worth considering spending a few extra dollars for a quality motherboard.

A quality motherboard is probably the item that will save you the most money in the end if you spend a bit more money initially. A high quality motherboard will usually have lots of room for upgrading your computer as a whole.

> ➢ Motherboard replacement for laptops is much more difficult and expensive than for a desktop computer. The reason for this is that most laptop motherboards are specifically designed for a certain case and model, and specific models are not manufactured over a long period of time. Even the best laptops do not have the same upgrade capabilities as a desktop computer.

If you are thinking about purchasing a laptop computer then you need to read the pros and cons section of purchasing a laptop that I have written here in my book. For the first point below, I am assuming that you are purchasing a desktop computer, not a laptop since laptop computers do not use PCI slots.

- As of today's standards, I highly recommend purchasing motherboards that have at least 4 PCI[3] slots.

- Most desktop computer motherboards, whether high quality or low-end quality, usually have at least two integrated components. (E.G. The video card, sound card, or the network card.)

If you are on a relatively low budget, you can purchase a low-end integrated motherboard that has all of the basic components built in. However, the problem with these types of boards is that since you have very few PCI slots (sometimes only 2), you do not have much room for upgrading or adding components. Moreover, the built-in components are not always high quality. You may also find that these types of boards also have very few USB connections as well.

A high quality desktop computer motherboard usually has a fair number of components built-in, an AGP slot for a high-end video card, at least four PCI slots, four or more USB slots, the ability to accept SATA[4] hard drives, the ability to accept DDR 2[5] memory, and the ability to handle additional USB ports.

---

[3] A PCI slot is a connector located on your computers motherboard that allows you to add additional components to your computer. PCI slots vary in size and in performance capability.
[4] SATA is also referred to Serial ATA. It is a hard drive connection interface technology. This refers to the type of connector used and the amount of data that can be processesd per second. Other hard drive connection interface technologies that exist today are IDE and SCSI.

> ➢ Make sure that your motherboard supports the processor and memory that you want to use. Not all motherboards support the same hardware components (in terms of CPU's and memory, etc). Check your motherboard's documentation to see which components it supports.

Many gamers like the performance of motherboards that use the *AMD* processor. It seems to work well and is generally a bit cheaper than *Intel* processors. However, that's not to say that *Intel* is a poor quality and over priced chip because for some applications it can out perform *AMD* by a slight margin. I personally find that *Intel* works well for games too. They are both comparable in terms of quality and performance. Keep in mind that the technology changes all the time, so capabilities increase and prices fluctuate.

## Motherboard Considerations:

You may want to upgrade your computer in the future, so you should make sure that your motherboard has the capability to accept a good range of upgrades so that you do not need to replace the motherboard in the near future just to perform an upgrade.

The most common components to upgrade are the CPU, memory, hard drive, and the video card.

To determine if your motherboard can accept certain upgrades, you will have to look at your motherboard's manual, research your particular motherboard make and model on the Internet, or in the case of a brand name computer, you can search the company's web site for your computer model.

I would recommend that you purchase a computer with a motherboard that has at least four PCI slots and four *USB slots available for adding additional devices. The PCI slots are located on your motherboard and cannot be added or removed because they are embedded into the motherboard. The PCI rule-of-thumb does not apply to laptop computers, however, because laptops do not use PCI slots. Instead, they use USB and PCMCIA slots[6].

Ensuring that your computer is upgradeable is essential. I have seen computer motherboards that have only one PCI slot, and only two memory slots available, stay

---

[5] DDR memory is double data rate memory that comes in the form of rectangular electronic board that is approximately 1 inch high and 3 to 5 inches wide. It is much faster than memory used previously by Pentium 3 and earlier computers because it processes much more data per second.
[6] A PCMCIA slot is an external slot on a laptop that allows you to add additional devices, such as an external CD-ROM, floppy drive, or network card.

away from these systems because they obviously do not give you much room for future upgrades. If you are going to want to upgrade a computer system in the future, it makes sense to purchase something upgradeable.

Consider the following characteristics of a motherboard:

- How many PCI slots it has (except laptops)
- How many USB connections it has
- The type of processors it accepts
- How much RAM memory can be added to it
- The types of RAM memory it does accept
- How many and what type of integrated components it does have (Remember that integrated components are often not the same quality as some non-integrated components.
- Whether it has a built-in Ethernet network card.
- If it has onboard SATA hard drive connections
- If it is a 32 or 64 bit motherboard
- The speed of the *Front Side Bus

If you are still unsure about how to find your motherboard information, ask a salesperson or a technician. If they cannot provide you with this information, let the buyer beware.

## Monitors:

New computer monitors manufactured today are flat screen LCDs (Liquid Crystal Displays). This is the technology that laptop computer monitors use. The older types of monitors are CRT (Cathode-Ray Tube) monitors which look similar to television sets.

CRT monitors generally have a better quality image than LCD monitors, but they are becoming more rare as LCD flat screen monitors are taking over the market in stores. In addition, the LCD image quality is getting better all the time. Probably by the time you read this book, LCD image quality will meet or exceed that of the CRT monitors.

- The typical life of a computer monitor is five to seven years.

When you are purchasing an LCD monitor, here are some things to look for:

(1) **You need to consider the dot pitch.** The dot pitch represents the amount of space between dots on your screen. The lower the dot pitch, the better the image. This is because you get more dots per inch in each square inch.

(2) **You should consider the contrast ratio.** If you try to view an LCD monitor with a low contrast ratio at a side angle the image will not be very good. You tend to get better images on LCD monitors with a contrast ratio of 600:1 or higher (i.e. 800:1)

(3) **The response time is also important.** This refers to the amount of time that it takes for an image to appear on the screen. The lower the response time, the faster the image shows up. If you ever use an LCD monitor with a high response time you will know what I mean when you move your mouse; you will see and practically feel the delay in the movement of your mouse cursor on the screen. I highly recommend that you get an LCD monitor with a response time of 8 ms (milliseconds) or less.

## Video Cards:

The video card is the component of your computer that connects your monitor to your computer so that you can see graphics on your screen. Sometimes this component is integrated within the motherboard, but a separate video card is usually used on higher end home computers (with the exception of most servers[7] and laptop computers). The reason for this is that non-integrated video cards are usually much more powerful.

For a gaming, multimedia, or graphic design system you will need a relatively high-end video card. As of November 2007, higher end video cards generally cost upwards of $150 and usually come with at least four cache pipelines[8] with at least 256 megabytes of DDR (Double Data Rate) memory. Of course, the more cache pipelines and memory, the better. If you can afford it initially and you want to save money in the end, you will probably want to purchase a top end video card so that you will not have to replace it for a while. For a few extra dollars, you can usually get something that has twice the amount of memory.

---

[7] A server is another computer that provides a service to users and other computers. Examples include an Internet server computer that provides you access to the Internet, an email server that allows you to send and receive email, and a web server that provides you with pages to Internet web sites.
[8] A cache pipeline is an electronic bus on the video card that provides a connection between the video card's memory and central processing unit.

➢ If you are purchasing the *Microsoft Vista* operating system, you will want to purchase a video card with at least 128 megabytes of DDR memory, anything less will likely not work properly.

• High-end non-integrated video cards come with their own central processing unit and DDR memory, which of course helps take a load off the main system memory and central processing unit.

If you require a mid or high-end video card, then you need to consider the following:

➢ Amount of memory it has
➢ Speed of its own central processing unit
➢ The number of cache pipelines it has
➢ The memory bus width (these days 256 bits is common).
➢ Whether or not it has support for the *Microsoft DirectX 9.0* (or higher) standard.

• Video cards not integrated with the motherboard typically use a special AGP (Accelerated Graphics Port) slot on the motherboard, or they use a PCI Express slot. It is not very common these days to use PCI video cards (this is not the same as PCI Express).

Almost all new motherboards for desktop computers have the AGP video card slot, however, many motherboards manufactured in the 1990s and early 2000s may not have this slot. If your computer does not have a special AGP slot, then you will have to use a video card that uses a PCI or PCI Express slot located on your computers motherboard, or a motherboard with an integrated video card. To sum it up, if your new motherboard does not have an AGP or PCI Express slot, then it is either a server motherboard or it is old technology.

• Many motherboards designed for high-end commercial servers do not have AGP slots.

• ATI and NVIDIA are well-known high-end video card manufacturers.

• PCI Express and AGP video cards are of a much higher quality than PCI or integrated video cards. They are usually faster, have more memory, more cache pipelines, and can be used in most computers currently manufactured.

14

For basic users who want to do little more than write word documents, send email, and surf the Internet then a motherboard with an integrated video card, network card, and other integrated components should work fine for you.  Currently, most integrated video cards do not exceed 64MB of memory, but you should not need anything more in this particular case (unless of course you are running *Microsoft Vista*).

> ➢ Remember, laptop computers do not have AGP, PCI, or PCI express slots, so you cannot add these types of vide cards to laptop computers.

## Sound Cards:

A sound card is the device that provides your computer with sound capability.

Most computer motherboards come manufactured with sound cards.  Depending on the quality of the motherboard, you may actually find some motherboards with sound cards that are of high quality and built by a well-known name brand manufacturer.  Some of the higher quality sound cards have electronic data busses that are 64 bits or higher in size.

- PCI slot-based sound cards are usually higher quality than integrated sound cards.

Should you decide that you want to install a separate PCI sound card, you may have to have a computer technician disable the integrated sound card on your motherboard (if it has one) for your new sound card to work properly.  Non-integrated sound cards use one of the PCI slots on your computer's motherboard.  You normally disable integrated sound cards either through the computer's BIOS[9] settings or through jumper settings on the motherboard itself.  You should not have to do this with most computer motherboards manufactured in 2000 or later though, however, consider yourself warned.

- *Creative* ([www.creative.com](http://www.creative.com)) is a company that is well known for producing quality sound cards and related products.

Like video cards, the type of sound card you will want to choose depends on your needs and how much money you can afford to spend.  If you are building a gaming system or

---

[9] The BIOS is a special program resides on a chip located on the motherboard.  It contains a very basic hardware configuration and set of instructions used for starting your computer.

media center, or if sound quality is a major concern for you, then you will probably be spending over $100 for a quality sound card. This is not to say that anything below $100 is poor quality, but the high-end sound cards do typically cost over $100. Quality sound cards should have surround-sound capability as well.

- Different sound cards will have different capabilities. It never hurts to look at the specifications and do some comparisons between different makes and models to see what each one has to offer.

## Speakers:

The speakers, like the video and sound cards, vary in quality. What type you will purchase depends on what you will be using them for, and how much money you can afford to spend.

- If you plan on purchasing a more expensive, quality sound card, then you might as well get good quality speakers, otherwise you will have wasted your money and will not see much of a difference in the quality of sound.

Quality speaker systems usually cost in excess of fifty dollars in Canadian funds, and they come with at least one sub-woofer and two regular speakers, a volume control, and a power adapter. Usually the volume control is located on one of the speakers. However, some speaker systems have remote control capability. Some sets may come with four or five speakers for surround-sound capability

Many computer shops carry the smaller ten-dollar pairs of speakers, but you should only consider these if sound quality is not important to you. If you are a gamer or someone who likes watching movies on your computer then you probably would not be happy with these types of speakers.

- When shopping for speakers, see if the store will let you listen to them before making a purchase. You do not want to buy something and then find out later that it is not what you want.

**<u>Network or Ethernet Cards:</u>**

The network card is the device that provides your computer with high-speed network and Internet access.

There are wireless and wire-based network cards. The wire-based network cards have either a large telephone-like jack, or a television-like cable connector. In almost all cases, they have the telephone-like jack that has eight pins instead of the television cable connector. Wireless network cards generally do not come with a jack as mentioned above, but this could change in the future.

- Most new laptop and desktop computer motherboards come with a wire-based network card built-in, which is sufficient for most users.

- Some laptop computers also come integrated with a wireless network card.

For a home desktop computer you can purchase a *D-link*, *Linksys*, or *Netgear* PCI network card from either *Staples/Business Depot* or *Futureshop* for approximately twenty dollars or less. However, for a laptop computer you should expect to pay a little bit more money for a network card if your laptop does not have one that is already integrated. There are other brands out there, but for compatibility reasons I would recommend that you stay with the top brand names. This is especially true when it comes to wireless network cards.

- ➤ Here is a quick tip: If you are building a wireless network, you should stay with the same brand name for each device when purchasing your wireless router and your wireless network cards. A couple of reasons for this are compatibility and support. If a wireless network card and router are from different brands, there is no guarantee that they will work well together. In addition, for support purposes, it would be easier if you just had to call one manufacturer for technical support on both devices.

- If you are using a wired network, make sure that the network card meets current standards. By this, I mean find out what speeds it supports by looking at the back of the card near the port that looks like a large telephone jack, on the product packaging, manufacturer web site, or in the product manual if you have access to it. If you do not see a number shown as 10/100 or 10/100/1000, then do not use that network card because it is probably old technology and therefore only supports connection speeds of up to 10 megabits per second. On the other hand, if it displays 10/100 or 10/100/1000, then it meets more current standards and will likely work well. Of course, you should be safe if you purchase a brand new card from a well-known computer store.

- If you are a laptop user and you have an integrated wireless network card, you still may need to purchase a non-integrated wireless network card for reasons mentioned above and because sometimes the other electronics inside the computer can cause interference with an internal card. I have seen cases where integrated wireless network cards could not communicate with wireless routers that were only three feet away because of both interference and compatibility issues.

## Keyboards:

Keyboards can range in price anywhere from $10 and higher. It is common to pay $30 or more for a quality keyboard. I have used cheap keyboards and have found that my typing ability decreases and the keys break much more easily. Would you mind having to purchase a new keyboard every two months, or would you rather purchase something that will last you a long time?

Some keyboards come with special function keys that integrate with the *Microsoft Windows* operating system and various programs. For example, it is common to find keys for the calculator, logging off, viewing pictures, opening your email, volume control, and a host of other options. However, you will not find most of these options on cheap keyboards that cost less than $10.

If you plan to use your computer a lot, then get either an ergonomic keyboard or a keyboard with a wrist rest. You do not want to risk developing Carpel Tunnel Syndrome. Trust me, I am talking from experience.

- Most new keyboards use USB[10] type connections.

- The beauty of using USB technology is that you can unplug and plug in USB devices while the computer is still running. If you are using a *Mac* or *Windows*-based system, your computer should automatically detect and install the device. The same will likely hold true for many *Linux*[11] distributions in the near future as well I am sure.

---

[10] USB stands for Universal Serial Bus. This is a high-speed technology that allows you to connect and disconnect hardware devices while your computer is turned on.
[11] Linux is a free open source operating system and operates in a similar manner to Microsoft Windows. Due to it's robustness, it is often found on various types on Internet servers.

> For non-USB devices, you should never unplug them or plug them in while your computer is on. Doing this could damage your computer. Make sure you turn off your computer before removing or adding these devices. This also goes for all types of internal hardware components as well.

## Central Processing Unit (The Processor):

The processor is the brain of your computer; it does almost all of the processing of computer code. Your computer cannot function without it. It, along with the motherboard, controls and performs almost all of your computers functions.

You can easily identify the Central Processing Unit because it is located on the motherboard and usually has a fan or a water-cooling system that covers it. On some older systems, the CPU attaches to a board that fits into a slot on the motherboard that is slightly bigger than a PCI slot. Newer processors attach directly to the motherboard.

In today's markets, new processors range in speeds and prices depending on the manufacturer, speed, number of processor cores, and the amount of cache memory available on the processor. Some gamers like to use *AMD*[12] processors, while others like to use *Intel*-based processors. Supposedly, *AMD* processors handle some large computer games in a better fashion than *Intel* processors. I have used both *AMD* and *Intel* and they both have worked well for the most part.

Current processors have multi-core technology. This is like having multiple Central Processing Units in one, effectively enhancing the performance for many computer applications.

> Make sure the processor that you want to use supports the motherboard that you want to use it with, and vice-versa. For example, if you want to use an *AMD* processor, then your motherboard must support *AMD* and the particular processor model that you are interested in using.

> Until recently, *Apple Mac* computers have used proprietary central processing units and many other non-standard hardware components, which will not work on other personal computers that use *Intel* and *AMD*, based hardware. This meant that you could not expect to be able to install the *Windows* operating system on *Macintosh* specific hardware.

---

[12] AMD, like Intel, is a manufacturer of Central Processing Units.

- It is common to find *Mac* computers that have all of the core hardware combined, that is, the CPU box, keyboard, and monitor built into one.

- *Apple* is currently selling *Mac* computers that use an *Intel* based hardware configuration.

## Computer Case:

This houses all of your inner computer components.

Cases generally come with a power supply unit, although some cases require you to purchase the power supply separately.

All cases serve the same purpose, but prices can range to over $100 if you want a fancy case with a high quality power supply. Cheaper cases with a power supply sometimes sell for approximately $40. Some of the more expensive cases may contain front panels for various connections, such as USB, flashcards, and speakers. Depending on your needs, a more expensive case may actually save you money in the end if it already has the components that you need.

## Power Supply Units:

Besides laptops, some *Mac* computers, and the odd brand name computer, power supply units are usually a standardized item that will fit inside most computer cases and work with most computer motherboards. You can find standardized power supply units at most computer stores.

Most generic brands do not provide a consistent level of power. For example, a generic power supply rated for 400 watts may not put out 400 watts as soon as you hit the power switch, instead, it may operate on an on-demand basis. In other words, the most that it will put out is the amount that it is rated to put out if your system demands the power at any one point.

- ➢ A good quality power supply will produce its rated amount immediately because it has higher quality components. You might be surprised how much a high-end power supply can do for your desktop computer system in terms of performance.

> ➢ Laptops have power supplies that are non-standardized. This means that you normally cannot use them on different systems.

Cheap power supplies cost approximately $20-$30. Higher quality power supplies usually cost more than $50, and some of the newer ones come with additional fans for better system cooling.

> ➢ You can usually tell the difference between a quality and a cheap power supply simply by weighing the two in your hand. A higher quality power supply usually weighs more because it has more inner-components.

> • New power supplies (with the exception of laptops) will generally fit inside any case designed for an *Intel Pentium 3, Pentium 4, or AMD* processor and motherboard, unless of course the computer is not standardized.

All new *AMD* and *Intel Pentium 4* (with the exception of some brand name systems), generally all *Pentium 3*, and some *Pentium 2* computers use a physical form factor called ATX[13]. Some older systems use the AT form factor. If you have bought a *Pentium 3* computer from a store then most likely it is in the ATX form factor. Do not get confused. Some Pentium 2 AT form factor motherboards had the ability to be upgraded to *Pentium 3* processor compatibility simply by updating the computers BIOS program, this does not transform them into ATX motherboards.

> • The difference between AT and ATX is the physical design of the component.

> ➢ To find a power supply that fits an AT form factor case, you will likely have to find one at a second-hand parts shop, or take one out of an old AT form factor computer. Simply put, companies no longer manufacture them.

> ➢ Make sure you confirm your purchases with the sales person. For example, confirm whether you are purchasing an "on-demand" or a pure power supply. If the sales person simply tells you, "don't worry, it will do what you want it to do", then they are trying to avoid answering your question. Consider taking your business elsewhere, as good salesperson will be honest with you.

---

[13] ATX is a technology that describes the physical design of a computer case, motherboard, and power supply unit. Concisely, if you are going to use an ATX-based motherboard, then your computer case and power supply must be designed to support the ATX form factor.

➤ If you are purchasing a second-hand *Pentium 2* or *Pentium 3* computer, try to find out the form factor of the power supply. If you have to replace the power supply, then you will know what you need to get and where to look.

• *Antec* and *Enermax* are two examples of companies that produce high-end power supply units.

## Main Memory:

Plain and simple, your computer will not operate without main memory.

The memory sticks in your computer are easy to identify. They are approximately 1 inch in height and usually 4 to 5 inches in length and have a long row of metal teeth at the bottom. They also connect directly to your computers' motherboard since they have their own special slots.

➤ Make sure that your memory sticks have gold plated teeth. These sticks conduct electricity more efficiently and therefore the computers performance is enhanced.

Main Memory Key Points:

❑ Main memory is cheaper than cache memory so your computer can have lots of it at a low price.
❑ Main memory is not quite as fast as cache memory.
❑ Main memory is still much faster than accessing the hard drive.
❑ Main memory temporarily stores parts of the operating system inside itself while the computer is operating to enhance performance.
❑ In addition, it also temporarily stores programs and other sorts of files that you access so it allows for faster access.
❑ Unlike cache memory, constant refreshment is required, so files are not stored in memory for a long length of time.
❑ Like cache memory, main memory is erased when you shut down the computer.

Older forms of memory are known as SIMM's (Single In-line Memory Modules) and DIMM (Dual In-line Memory Module) SD-RAM (Synchronous Dynamic RAM). Newer computers use DDR (Double Data Rate) memory.

> DDR and SD-RAM chips look identical and use identical looking slots on the motherboard, however, they are not interchangeable and you should never try to use both types of RAM at the same time. Doing so could damage the memory chips and your motherboard. Check your motherboard specifications to see what types of memory it will accept. If it accepts DDR memory, (New motherboards will accept this type of memory) find out exactly what type of DDR memory it does accept.

DDR SD-RAM operates at a faster speed than the older types of RAM and transmits many times more data per cycle.

Older SD-RAM used to operate at 66, 100, or 133 MHz. Common speeds for DDR RAM today are 266MHz, 333MHz, 400MHz, and 433MHz. Higher speeds known as DDR2 and DDR3 are being developed as this book is being written. Current DDR2 speeds are exceeding 667MHz. Again, check your motherboards documentation to see what your motherboard supports in terms of memory and other components.

• IF your budget allows for it, I strongly recommend obtaining the faster RAM, so you will not have to upgrade your memory often. It is somewhat pointless to purchase a system that you will have to upgrade in 3 months.

• It is very difficult to purchase older SD-RAM in stores now because this technology is outdated.

## Mouse:

A mouse is the pointing device most often used for clicking on icons and various program components for your computer. It is also one of the simplest components to install on a computer. Most mice today connect to your computer by means of a USB port so that you can just plug it in and start using it for the most part. You may have to install mouse drivers if you are using a *Windows* operating system earlier than *Windows XP*.

> Stay away from the old track-ball mice. [14]Optical mice stay cleaner and last much longer, and you can get one at any computer shop for fifteen dollars or less. You

---

[14] Optical mice use an infrared light at the bottom of the mouse to track mouse movement. Therefore, no trackball is required, resulting in cleaner and more efficient mouse usage.

also do not need a mouse pad for optical mice either; they will work on almost any type of surface.

- If you have limited room on your desk for using your mouse, you can purchase mice that are half the size of a regular mouse. Additionally, on most operating systems, you can adjust the mouse speed so that you do not have to move the mouse very far to move the cursor to where you want it on your computer screen.

Optical mice are identified by the light that shines on the bottom. In addition, they do not have a ball at the bottom.

## Operating Systems:

An operating system is the main piece of software that must be installed on all computers. It allows users to interact with their computer hardware and software, and it allows software to interact with hardware and computer users and so on. Without some form of an operating system, your computer will not function.

- Whether or not you know it, all forms of electronics have some form of operating system installed in them.

For more information about operating systems, please refer to the section called *The King of Software, The Operating System*.

## Anti-virus Software:

Without anti-virus software, you will eventually get computer viruses, no doubt about it. This is especially true if you use the *Microsoft Windows* operating system, which is the most commonly used computer operating system today.

There are plenty of good anti-virus software programs out there. *McAfee*, *AVG* (www.grisoft.com) and *Panda Software* tend to do good jobs at finding and destroying most viruses.

➤ With new viruses coming out each day, no anti-virus product is up-to-date when you purchase it from the store. You need to run the on-line update utility that comes with each anti-virus product to ensure that your program and virus definition database is up-to-date.

➤ Make sure you configure your antivirus software to update automatically, scan email messages for viruses, and to do in-depth scanning of all of your files for viruses.

➤ If you are not sure what product to purchase then you should seek the help of a non-biased technician or consultant. You can also ask friends and co-workers about products they use, but beware, if they tell you that they never have any viruses, it may be because their anti-virus program simply is not able to detect them. A good antivirus program will alert you immediately when it detects a virus.

• As a side note, I have seen some common anti-virus programs literally bring some brand new computer systems literally to the speed of a turtle going up a hill on a cold winter's day. If you install an anti-virus product and this happens to you, try un-installing your anti-virus program and then re-installing it. If this still does not work then un-install your anti-virus program and try another piece of anti-virus software.

➤ While there are some good on-line virus scanning utilities, such as Panda Software's Activescan Pro (www.pandasoftware.com), they should never be used as an antivirus program replacement for the simple fact that you do not get consistent real time protection for the whole time that your computer is turned on. The only time these programs run is when you manually run them from their web site. You will not be protected if you do not have an antivirus program that operates on your computer the moment you turn it on.

➤ Viruses can spread rapidly and you cannot always repair a damaged file. Make sure you have a good antivirus program and a good data backup strategy.

➤ If I have not scared you enough, read the section of this book called *Security Sense*.

## Spy-ware, Ad-ware, Browser Hi-jack, and Mal-ware Removal Software:

You should not confuse spy-ware, ad-ware, browser hi-jack software, and some forms of mal-ware with viruses. Most, and I mean most, anti-virus software alone will not search for and destroy these other nasty pests. These pests can be installed on your computer at any time without you knowing it and are commonly installed by the simple act of visiting certain web sites, and downloading and installing free or non-reputable software, music, and videos from rogue sites and programs.

> Probably the worst kind of program that you can install on your computer is a file sharing program. These programs allow you to connect to other computers and download music, videos, and other types of files from other computers. After all, you do not know what kinds of nasty critters live on other people's computers. You could be downloading one file from ten computers, and if one of those computers is infected with a virus, then you most likely have just contracted the virus.

> Oh yes, and stay away from the pornography and gambling sites too!

I highly suggest that you install more than one utility to remove spy-ware, ad-ware, and mal-ware as different utilities scan your computer in different ways and find different infections.

- Four such utilities that I use are *Ad-aware*, *Spy-bot Search & Destroy*, *AVG Anti-spy-ware*, and *Spy-ware Doctor by Pctools.com (www.pctools.com)*. The paid version of *Spy-ware Doctor* consistently runs in the background and has a lot of functionality.

Please read the security section called *Security Sense* for more information about these nuisances, you will find some good information there.

## Hard Drive:

The hard drive is the component inside your computer that stores all of your programs, files, and information. Your computer is virtually useless without one of these.

Most new hard drives manufactured today have at least 300 gigabytes of storage.

Hard drives are one of the slower hardware components inside of a computer, so you should consider the following when purchasing a new hard drive, or a new computer for that matter:

➢ Consider how many RPMs (Revolutions per Minute) the hard drive can spin at on average. If it can spin faster, then it can send and receive data faster. Current standard IDE desktop hard drives operate at a speed of at least 7200 revolutions per minute.

➢ How much cache memory does the hard drive have? Modern hard drives have at least 8 megabytes of cache memory, but some newer drives come with 16 megabytes of cache memory, which is even better.

- I can remember swapping a hard drive with 2 megabytes of cache memory to one with 16 megabytes of cache memory for one of my regular customers, and I could see a huge difference in performance. This was on a Pentium 2 system. After I installed the new hard drive, his Pentium 2 system was then comparable in performance to his Pentium 4 system.

➢ What form of hard drive are you using? Is it ATA, Serial ATA, or SCSI (pronounced skuzzy)?

Serial ATA has a higher data transmission rate then the standard ATA hard drive form. Out of the three, SCSI 160 and 320 has the best performance, but these drives usually require a SCSI controller card, and these components may be cost restrictive. Serial ATA does out-perform standard ATA for the most part and generally does not require a special controller card, unless your motherboard does not already have a built-in Serial ATA card.

Obviously, the higher performance drive you want, the more you are going to have to pay. However, SATA (Serial ATA) is only a bit more expensive than standard ATA technology. Some SCSI implementations can cost as much as an entire computer system.

I do highly recommend that you read my section called *The King of Storage: The Hard Drive* as it goes into further details about hard drives.

## CD-ROM:

Most new standard CD-ROM devices operate at a speed of 52x. These devices have become quite inexpensive over the years. You can purchase one in almost any computer shop for approximately $20. The "x" stands for 150 kilobytes of data per second. Therefore, the transfer speed of a 52x CD-ROM would be 52 times 150.

- Most software today comes on a CD or DVD-ROM.

## CD-Burner:

New CD-Burners these days have three actions: recording, rewriting, and reading. In the example of a CD-Burner with a rating of 52x48x52, the burner has the capability to burn at 52 X 150 kilobytes per second, re-write at 48 X 150 kilobytes per second, and read at 52 X 150 kilobytes per second.

## DVD Player:

DVD's look like CD's, but are a much higher quality medium than CDs and can hold at least 8 times the amount of data that a CD can hold. DVD players read DVD's at a higher rate than what a CD player will read a CD.

You can also play CDs with DVD players as well.

## DVD Burner:

DVD burners are probably your best deal. For a few dollars more than a DVD player, you can buy a DVD burner combo drive, which plays and burns DVDs and can act as a CD-ROM and CD-Burner as well. This is what I would recommend for most users.

- Some high-end DVD burner combo drives can cost over 5 times the price of a CD-Burner. One such example are DVD burners manufactured by *Plextor*.

Beware: like you should for all of your computer components, make sure you purchase this from a shop that deals with known good quality manufacturers that will give you good support if you need it. I am sure that I do not have to tell you that you want something that is going to last you a long time.

To compare DVDs against CDs, please see the following chart. In simple terms, the higher the number, the better the quality.

**DVD's vs. CD's**

| Specification | CD Audio | DVD Audio |
|---|---|---|
| Sampling Rate | 44.1 KHz | 192 kHz |
| Samples Per Second | 44,100 | 192,000 |
| Sampling Accuracy | 16 bits per sample | 24 bits per sample |
| Number of Possible Outputs | 65,536 | 16,777,216 |

**<u>Scanners:</u>**

A scanner is the optical device that translates images into file formats that computers can understand. Scanners will not differentiate between images and text, so unfortunately you cannot scan a document and then save it as a text file for editing (not yet anyway).

- To increase the quality of an image, you need to scan the image at a high DPI (Dots per Inch) resolution setting.

➤ Remember that higher quality images have a larger file size and take longer to open. While the length of time to open an image is not usually noticeable on new computers, it can be noticeable on some older computers designed before the Pentium 4 era or that have low amounts of memory. Even these days with the consistent advancement of technology, you do not get something for nothing.

Typical optical scanners support a resolution of at least 600 DPI, while high-end scanners support a much higher resolution. Of course, like all electronic components, you will have to pay more for the high-end technology.

➤ New scanners typically use a USB connection to a USB port on your computer. Some computers built before the Pentium 3 may not have USB ports or USB capability, and unfortunately, most new scanners these days only allow for a USB connection. It is possible to purchase scanners that give you the option to use a network connection, but they are not as common and selections are more limited.

> ➢ I know that I am beginning to sound like a parrot who constantly repeats itself, but check to make sure that your system will support the components that you want to use before you waste your time and money buying something that you cannot use. If you are not sure what you are doing, talk to someone you can trust.

## Printers:

The type of printer that you will choose should depend on what you are going to be printing and the size of your wallet.

> ➢ If you are going to be printing color images then you will need to use an ink-jet printer or a color laser printer.

> • If you are going to be printing important documents, such as resumes, then I would strongly suggest that you use a laser printer. That resume for your next job interview will look more professional if it is printed on a laser printer and, therefore, may get you that six-figure income that you want so badly. Do not bother with the color laser printer unless you are going to print important documents that require color.

Laser printers initially are much more expensive than most ink-jet printers are, but the cartridges last much longer. Therefore, you can save a lot of money in the end. Most ink-jet cartridges will print 200-400 pages, but laser printer cartridges usually last well over 1000 pages. Some laser printers that print only black can last up to 6000 pages and cost well under $200 CAD for a cartridge. The prices may change by the time you read this book, but the point is that you will save more money in the end by using a laser printer, and your documents will look more professional.

A color laser printer is more expensive than a black laser monochrome printer is. However, the image quality beats the ink-jet printers and the cartridges last much longer, so you will still save a lot more money in the end.

> • If you cannot afford multiple printer types, then ask yourself how much you can afford to spend, what is most important to you, and what you will print most often.

Like scanners, printers also use a DPI resolution rating; the higher the better quality. This brings up an important point: if you are scanning and then printing images from your computer, the quality of the printout will only be what the device with the lowest DPI rating is capable of or setup to put out. In other words, if you scan an image at 1200 DPI but you print it on a printer with a 600 DPI setting, your printout will only have a maximum quality of 600 DPI. After all, a chain is only as good as its weakest link.

- New printers typically use a USB connection to a USB port on your computer. Some computers built before the Pentium 3 systems may not have USB ports or USB capability, and typically use a [15]parallel port connection. Before purchasing a printer, check your computer's connection capabilities if you are unsure what you have. You will typically find the connectors in the back of your computer.

- High-end end printers sometimes have built-in network cards. This would allow any computer in a network to access the printer. The only requirement is that each computer would need to have the printer driver software installed. In a *Windows* environment where a computer is acting as a print server, the print server could hold all of the required drivers and most printer settings for each client computer. On the server, you can make the printer sharable so that each client would only have to logically search for the printer using *Windows* Explorer and then simply click on the printer icon to connect to it. Of course, the print server would have to be turned on (this sounds obvious, but you have no idea how many people forget this).

- For ink-jet printers, use your printer at least twice per week, or at least run the printer cleaning software to reduce the chance of your printer cartridges drying out. Unlike laser printer cartridges, if you do not use your cartridges, they will dry out. If your cartridge dries out then you may have to purchase a new cartridge, which are not cheap considering the amount of pages that they print in comparison to a laser printer. Laser printers do not have this problem because they operate in a very different fashion and actually do not use liquid ink. Instead, they use a powder-based toner.

### All-in-one devices or Multi-Function devices:

All-in-one devices generally consist of either three or more devices built into one unit, such as a fax machine, printer, scanner, copier, and slots for memory cards.

---

[15] A parallel port connection uses a D shaped connector with 25 pins. Although it is bigger and has more pins than a USB connector, it operates at a slower speed.

These devices are much cheaper to purchase than if you bought each device separately, and you usually do not need multiple cables connected to your computer. This frees up more space on your desk and connection ports on your computer.

Typically, these devices use standard ink-jet printer cartridges although some of the more expensive multi-function devices use laser printer cartridges, which last longer and provide better print quality.

- One important note about these devices is that when the device breaks, you will lose use of all your components during repair or replacement. This is fine if you are a home user and do not need consistent use of your multi-function device, but if you need to print important documents on a regular basis then it is a good idea to have a backup device (i.e. printer, scanner, fax machine) just in case something does go wrong.

- With the point above in mind, it is not usually worthwhile to try to repair all-in-one devices. Prices are coming down dramatically, so it is probably cheaper for you just to purchase a new device. Many technicians charge $50 or more per hour for servicing.

# The Brain & Speed Demon of the Computer: The Processor

**E**veryone these days is most concerned about the speed of the processor.

> The processor speed is important   However, in terms of performance you need to look at more than just the speed of the processor.  The CPU is one of many factors that affect performance.  You also need to consider the  following:

>> The speed of your motherboard's busses:  How fast is the front side bus that runs from your processor to your memory?

>> The type of RAM memory that you will use:  Are you using current DDR RAM, or are you just using the older and slower SD-RAM?

>> The speed and amount of processor cache memory.  Does your processor cache run at the same speed as your processor, or does it run at half the speed?  Do you have 1 MB of processor cache, or 512 KB?

>> Does the processor have more than one core?

>> The speed of your hard drive in terms of revolutions per minute!

>> The type of hard drive you are using:  Is it ATA, Serial ATA, or SCSI?  SCSI is currently the fastest, but most expensive technology!

>> Amount of cache memory on your hard drive!

>> The speed of your video card processor (if you are going to use a non-integrated video card)!

>> The bus size of your video cache pipelines (if you are going to use a non-integrated video card)!
>> The amount of memory that your video card possesses!

>> Again, the type of memory that your video card uses!  Current video cards use DDR memory.

>> System cooling:  How many fans do you have in your system?

The two major processor manufacturers today for home personal computers and servers are *AMD (Advanced Micro Devices)* and *Intel*. *Apple* used to manufacture most of their own hardware, including motherboards and central processing units, but have switched over to *Intel* hardware. All companies produce quality components at a high rate of performance.

Central Processing Units each have a processor core (at least one core).

- Today, *Intel* and *AMD* are developing newer processors that have two or more cores, which is virtually the same thing as having multiple Central Processing Units in one. This gives you more power and speed.

- Newer processors come with level 1, level 2, and now even level 3 cache. Level 1 cache is the fastest of the three. Level 2 cache typically runs at a slower speed than level 1, but typically has a higher storage capacity. The same idea holds true for the new level 3 cache. The speed and amount of cache will vary from processor to processor, and the price will vary as well as a result.

- ➤ While on the topic of central processing units, I also want to remind you that you cannot interchange *Intel, AMD*, and *Apple* hardware components with each other. You have to go with what your motherboard is designed to support. Check your motherboard's specifications to see what it supports, or check with your sales person before purchasing.

- Many newer processors manufactured today also come with a bus size of 64 bits.

Many of the older processors use a 16-bit or 32-bit bus. A 64-bit processor with a speed of 3.0 GHz and 1 MB of cache that runs at core speed will run faster a 32-bit processor that has the exact same speed and cache characteristics because it can process more data per cycle due to its increased bus size.

- ➤ To full take advantage of a 64-bit processor, your motherboard and operating system must definitely have 64-bit capability.

Of course, this is going to cost you more money. If you do not plan to purchase a 64-bit operating system, then do not waste your money on a 64-bit processor because you will not see much of a difference in performance.

## Multi-Core Technology:

Earlier in this section, I mentioned multi-core processor technology. Now let me talk about what multi-core technology is and about some of the other processor technologies that exist.

The core is the main component of the processor. Having multiple cores in one processor is essentially the same as having multiple processors. It gives your computer a much higher level of performance. Some users have mentioned that some applications have not taken full advantage of multi-core processors. You may or may not find that you will have to re-install some applications to take full advantage of the power of multi-core processors. Over all, you should still see quite a difference in performance between a single core and multi-core processor.

## Hyper-Thread technology:

This technology is found with *Intel Pentium* processors. Essentially, it is two virtual processors in one (but not two cores in one). This is obviously an improvement over previous processors, but it still does not have quite the same performance capability as the multi-core processors. This technology has been around slightly longer than multi-core processor technology.

## Centrino Processor Technology:

*Centrino* technology was developed by *Intel* to cope with issues such as power consumption, performance, heat, and wireless connectivity issues encountered with laptop computers and other portable devices. The chip itself runs slower than most processors, which results in less heat and less power consumption, but it has more cache memory than most other processors, therefore it can still outperform many faster processors designed for laptop computers.

As I mentioned previously, wireless connectivity enhancements are added to *Centrino* processors to enhance wireless connectivity to most standard wireless networks.

- The *Pentium M* processor (not to be confused with the older *Pentium 4 M*) is the processor that uses *Centrino* technology in laptops, and currently it only works in laptop computers.

- Current implementations of *Centrino* technology processors are also dual-core or multi-core.

In summary, the benefits of *Centrino* technology are:

➢ Longer battery life due to using a slower speed processor!
➢ Faster processing due to more processor cache memory!
➢ Better support for wireless networking!
➢ Less heat generated!

## Some Examples of Processors:

| Model | Manufacturer | Typical Speeds | Typical Amounts Of Cache |
|-------|--------------|----------------|--------------------------|
| Pentium | Intel | Lower than 233 MHz | 128 KB and Lower |
| Pentium MMX | Intel | Lower than 233 MHz | 128 KB and Lower |
| Pentium 2 | Intel | 233 to 400 MHz | 128 KB and higher |
| Pentium 3 | Intel | 450 MHz to 1.2 GHz | 256 KB and higher |
| Pentium 4 | Intel | 1 GHz and higher | 256 KB and higher |
| Pentium Celeron | Intel | Varies | Varies, lower than other Pentium processors |
| G4 | Apple Macintosh | Varies | Varies |
| G5 | Apple Macintosh | Varies | Varies |
| Athlon | AMD | Varies, but very high end | Varies |
| Athlon 64 | AMD | Varies, but very high end | Varies |
| Opteron | AMD | Varies, but very powerful | Varies |
| Sempron | AMD | Over 2 GHz | Varies |

# The King of Storage: The Hard Drive

**T**his component holds everything: all of your programs, your files, the operating system, and any data that you access and use on your computer that is not on any type of removable media. It is the storage device located inside your computer.

- The amount of storage space in today's new hard drives is measured in Gigabytes (GB). In the near future, it will be measured in Terabytes, as hard drive sizes increase on a regular basis.

Most brand new computers come with at least 200 Gigabytes of hard drive storage, which is currently more than enough for most home users. Hard drives with over 500 Gigabytes of storage space are now manufactured.

- To get an idea of the current standards, you should shop around and do some comparisons between systems. The amounts that I have given you are not written in stone as technology is constantly changing.

There are three main types of hard drive interfaces used today: ATA, Serial ATA, and SCSI (Small Computer System Interface, pronounced "skuzzy"). Each type of interface operates at a different speed, and like any other hardware component, the faster the speed, the higher the price, but the better the performance.

## ATA (Advanced Technology Attachment):

This type of a connection interface is also known as IDE (Integrated Drive Electronics). ATA hard drives are the most common, but the slowest of the three mentioned. This is not to say that they are slow as speeds are getting better all the time.

- ❑ These types of hard drives have their own on-board controller!
- ❑ They use a ribbon-like 40-pin cable that attaches your hard drive and CD or DVD devices to your computer!
- ❑ The cables used for ATA are referred to as either ATA or IDE (Integrated Drive Electronics) cables!
- ❑ Some cables have 40 pins and 80 wires to reduce electronic and electrical interference, thus improving performance!
- ❑ The most current ATA speeds allow data to be transferred at 133 Mega-bytes per second. This rate of speed is not guaranteed because speed also depends on the number of revolutions per minute (RPM) at which the hard drive spins at, the amount of cache memory the hard drive has, and a number of other factors.
- ❑ IDE cables can be up to 40 cm long. Anything longer will not work properly

## SATA (Serial Advanced Technology Attachment):

- ❑ Unlike ATA, SATA only uses four wires instead of 40, thus reducing electronic and electromechanical interference. Also, you have more room inside of your case due to the smaller wires.
- ❑ SATA only requires 250 millivolts (mV), whereas ATA requires 5 volts of electricity to operate!
- ❑ 150 MB per second is the starting transfer rate for SATA, unlike ATA, which has a current maximum transfer rate of 133 MB per second. Faster SATA technologies are being developed as time goes on.
- ❑ Serial ATA cables can extend up to 1 meter, in contrast to ATA cables, which can only extend up to 40 cm in length.

## SCSI:

SCSI is currently the fastest hard drive technology that exists today, although SATA appears to be catching up.

- ❑ SCSI devices may be cost-prohibitive as the devices themselves are very expensive to purchase and require the use of a special SCSI device controller card (all of which can sometimes cost a few hundred dollars).
- ❑ Current specifications allow for data transfer rates of 320 MB per second!
- ❑ The cables may look similar to the standard ATA ribbon cables, but are sometimes more bulky.

The SCSI STANDARDS:

| Type | Bus Width (Bits) | Transfer Rate (MB Per Second) | Connector | Maximum Cable Length (in meters) |
|---|---|---|---|---|
| SCSI 1 | 8 | 5 | DB-25 | 6 |
| SCSI 2 | 8, 16 | 5 | C-50 | 6 |
| Fast SCSI | 8 | 10 | C-50 | 3 |
| Wide SCSI | 16 | 20 | C-68 | 3 |
| Wide Ultra-2 | 16 | 80 | C-68 | 3 |
| Ultra SCSI | 8 | 20 | C-50 | 3 |
| Ultra 160 | 16 | 160 | C-68 | 12 |
| Ultra 320 | 16 | 320 | C-68 | 12 |

As you can see, there are many different types of SCSI interfaces. For most home users, either ATA or SATA will be more than sufficient.

SCSI is rarely used for a basic home computer, instead, it is most often found in Internet or network servers.

When shopping for a hard drive, consider these specifications:

(1) How many revolutions per minute the hard drive spins at!

(2) How much cache memory the hard drive has: Cache can make quite a noticeable difference!

(3) How much storage space the hard drive has!

(4) The type of hard drive technology that that the device uses (i.e. ATA, SATA, or SCSI)!

# The King of Software: The Operating System

Operating systems carry the most basic (but not all) hardware drivers for your motherboard and its components so that your computer can operate at a basic level. They also contain basic software components that allow users to perform system functions such as drawing pictures, writing text messages, accessing the Internet, and allowing users to perform very basic system maintenance.

- If you are using a new operating system and are installing an older piece of hardware, the operating system CD may have the necessary driver software for your hardware to function properly.

All electronic components carry some type of operating system. Even electronic medical emergency equipment uses some type of operating system to control its functions and give it functionality.

Some common operating systems in use today are *Microsoft Windows, Macintosh, Solaris, UNIX,* and the many variants of *Linux,* which is a derivative of the *UNIX* operating system. These are not the only operating systems that exist, but are the most common ones used at home and in business.

Both *UNIX* and *Linux* were originally designed to perform as server operating systems and are found on most Internet or network servers today. When you connect to the Internet, you will surely connect to a *UNIX* or *Linux* machine at some point, and you will not necessarily know it. To an end user on a remote computer, a web page will probably look the same whether or not it exists on a *Windows, Linux,* or *UNIX* based web server.

One of the biggest complaints about *UNIX* and *Linux* over the years has been that they are not user friendly. However, *UNIX* and *Linux* have become very graphical and more user friendly, so more home users are starting to use Linux at home. *UNIX* is rarely used on home computers.

Currently, most versions of *Linux* are open source, meaning that they are free for download and installation; however, obtaining technical support may be more costly because there are fewer technicians for *Linux* than for *Microsoft Windows,* and a fair bit of knowledge and skill is required to troubleshoot these systems. However, *Linux* trained technicians can usually work out issues with *Linux* in a short period of time due to the abundance of knowledge and resources available. You are probably asking yourself how *Linux* developers make a living. Many of them make a living by charging fees for support and writing education books.

Since *UNIX* and *Linux* were originally designed to run on servers, they are extremely stable and very powerful, however, they do not currently have the same level of hardware support that *Microsoft* has, although hardware support is improving each day for these operating systems. Because *Microsoft Windows* is the most commonly used operating system for home users, developers generally will develop software drivers for *Microsoft Windows* before any other type of operating system. However, *Linux* does support a large amount of hardware. Who knows, by the time you read this book, hardware driver support may be equivalent to that of *Microsoft Windows*.

- For those who do not know, a driver is a piece of software that controls a hardware component, and it must be separately developed for each specific operating system and each piece of hardware.

- ➢ Remember, before purchasing a piece of computer hardware, make sure that it has current drivers to support your computers operating system; otherwise, it will not work properly. For example, if you are using *Windows Vista* and the driver list on the hardware box does not list support for *Windows Vista*, you should search for another piece of computer hardware that supports *Vista*. If you are lucky and knowledgeable enough to install driver software on your own, you can try searching the hardware manufacturer's web site for the particular make and model of hardware you plan to purchase to see if they have the proper driver software for the hardware.

The same concepts hold true for general software as well. Your software has to be written for specific operation systems. Check the software box to see what operating systems it will operate on, or check the software vendor's web site for software that will operate correctly with your operating system. *Linux* operating system CDs tend to come with a huge abundance of quality open source software equivalent to many programs designed for the *Microsoft* operating system, and will usually run on any type of system, new or old.

- Some versions of *Linux* come with as many as 7 CD's worth of software including the operating system itself.

- If you want to learn how to use Linux on a *Microsoft Windows* computer, there is a version of *Linux* called *Knoppix* that runs entirely off the CD. You just need to put the CD inside your CD-ROM and restart your computer, provided that your computer is configured to start off CD-ROM before starting off your hard drive. This will allow you to learn *Linux* without affecting your existing installation of *Microsoft Windows*. *Linux* does not yet have support for all of *Microsoft's* hard drive file systems, namely the NTFS file system[16], so you may not be able to save files while using *Knoppix*. To load your computer back into *Windows*, simply reboot your computer, and during the process of rebooting, take out the *Knoppix* CD.

An alternative to this is to install a virtual PC program. These types of programs divide your computer in to multiple virtual computers. You load your operating system the way you normally would, run the virtual PC program, tell the program that you want to create a virtual PC, and then install the operating system when it prompts you for the disks. When all this is done, you can run multiple operating systems at the same time. The only drawback here is that you have to have a relatively powerful computer to handle multiple operating systems.

- When you are operating *Linux* from the CD, your computer will not allow you to remove the CD. You will need to restart your computer first. This is because the operating system is reading from the CD, and if you were able to remove the CD while running the operating system, the operating system would not be able to function.

- Any operating system that you install on your computer will usually come with basic software for functions such as email, text editing, web browsing, Internet connection setup, and basic system maintenance utilities (not anti-virus or anti-spyware utilities).

For advanced text editing, do not rely on the programs that come built into the operating system. They are usually very low end and do not have many capabilities. Your best bet is to obtain a software suite such as *Microsoft Office*, or Open Office. You will not be able to write a sharp looking resume with a basic text editor!

- Some of the newer operating systems are 64-bit systems. This allows for faster code execution, therefore enhancing system performance if your computers hardware is also 64-bit hardware. The idea here is that the electronic bus size is increased to 64 bits from 32 bits, so it can transfer more data in one cycle.

Older hardware and operating systems used 16 bit and 32-bit technology. This means that they will not take advantage of 64-bit configurations.

---

[16] A file system is a logical file structure setup by the operating system to provide needed functionality. An NTFS file system is a file system developed by Microsoft for Microsoft operating systems. Microsoft Windows NT, 2000, XP, and all Microsoft operating systems developed after Windows XP support the NTFS file system. NTFS provides security, enhanced performance, and additional capabilities over previous Microsoft file systems.

➢ To take full advantage of a 64-bit operating system, your motherboard and central processing unit must be able to operate in 64-bit mode. For example, if either your operating system or hardware can operate only at a level of 32-bits, then you will only get 32-bit performance.

# Sources for Finding Information

Through your days of computing, you will always have questions of sorts, no matter if you are a beginner, or an information technology expert.  Knowing where to find answers is important.  Here are some places where you can search for answers:

- On-line searches using key words
- Manufacturer web sites
- People with technical knowledge
- Technical books, like the one that you are reading now
- Specific technical books
- Technical magazines
- Experienced friends
- Knowledgeable co-workers
- Information technology professionals
- Consultants
- Internet chat forums, such as Usenet or browser based chat forums.

# Do I Want A Laptop or Desktop Computer?

No matter how you look at it, there are pro's and con's to whatever decision you make. While laptops are nice because of the portability, you really need to justify the costs and some of the risks involved.

| Some Pro's for New Laptop's | Some Con's for New Laptop's |
|---|---|
| Portable | More Expensive To Purchase |
| Light Weight | More Expensive To Repair |
| Generally As Fast As A Home Computer | More Difficult And Costly To Find A Technician For Hardware Repair Services |
| Built In Networking Devices Such As A Network Card, Modem, and Wireless Connection | More Easily Damaged Or Stolen. For example: Spilling Drinks On The Keyboard Or Leaving It Alone Accidentally When Someone Comes Along And Steals It |
| Good Battery Life | Replacement Parts Are Not Usually Manufactured For A Long Length Of Time |
| Built-In Devices Such As Sound Card, USB Connectivity, Printer Ports | Higher Potential For Hardware Malfunction Due To Overheating As A Result Of A Poor Air Circulation Due To A Tighter Enclosure |
| More Compact | More Limitations In Terms Of Adding Hardware |
| **Some Pro's for Home Computer's** | **Some Con's for Home Computer's** |
| Usually Less Expensive To Purchase | More Heavy Than A Laptop |
| Physically Easier To Replace Parts | Not Portable |
| Easier To Find A Technician | No Built-In Wireless Connection |
| Not As Easily Damaged Or Stolen | Takes Up More Desk Space |
| Less Expensive To Repair | |
| Built In Networking Devices Such As A Network Card, | |

| | |
|---|---|
| Modem | |
| Built-In Devices Such As Sound Card, USB Connectivity, Printer Ports | |
| Compatible Parts Are Manufactured For A Much Longer Period Of Time | |
| Less Prone To Overheating | |
| May Be Easy To Upgrade (If Your Motherboard Has The Capability) | |

> ➢ Remember, because of the physical hardware design of laptops, you cannot swap most internal hardware components between laptops and PCs.

If you can put a laptop to its intended use, then consider purchasing a laptop, if not then just go with the basic home computer and save yourself the money. Some good candidates for laptops are traveling business people, people who are on the road and need access to a computer, and students away at college or university.

- If you plan on purchasing a laptop and connecting to a wireless network, then you should purchase a laptop that has a processor that uses *Centrino* technology. Normally you can find this information by looking for an *Intel* sticker located on the laptop. For more information on *Centrino* technology, please see the section called "*The Brain & Speed Demon of The Computer: The Processor*".

# Should I Upgrade My Old Computer or Buy a New One?

**F**irst, ask yourself the following questions:

> ➤ How much can I afford to spend on upgrading?
> ➤ What exactly needs to be upgraded to enhance performance?
> ➤ What is the main problem with my current computer?
> ➤ How much can I afford to spend on a new computer?
> ➤ How well does my computer run compared to others that are newer and are running the same applications?
> ➤ How old is my computer?

If you plan to spend $700 on upgrading, consider putting that money towards a new computer.

- If your computer is more than four years old then it's not worth spending a lot of money on it to enhance performance. However, you can add additional devices for extra capabilities, such as printing, burning DVD's, or listening to music.

- If you are looking to upgrade your computer system, consider upgrading the slowest component first. In many cases, this is usually the hard drive. If you are unsure what component needs to be upgraded, have a computer technician assist you. Simply upgrading the hard drive may be enough to satisfy your needs.

## Don't Mix and Match Your Memory:

Remember, you may not be able to upgrade certain components with new components. Take RAM memory for example. Today's computer systems use DDR memory, while earlier systems use similar looking SD-RAM.

> ➤ Even though DDR RAM may physically fit into an SD-RAM slot, the two are not interchangeable, and you will likely damage your computer if you try to interchange these parts.

- Remember that your system is only really going to be as fast as its slowest component, so you should never use old hardware, memory, or processors inside new computers.

- Consider doing a baseline test to see what hardware components are the busiest. A computer technician should be able to assist you with this.

➤ When a new operating system is released, the programs on your old computer may not be able to support it.

➤ Remember that RAM memory holds common instructions and data so that the processor does not have to go to the hard drive to retrieve data and instructions as often. The more memory you have, the less busy your processor will be.

- If you are using *Windows 2000* or later, you can check your CPU and Memory usage by pressing the *<CTRL> <ALT> and <DELETE>* buttons all at the same time. You can then press the *Task Manager* button, which will show you what programs and processes are running on your computer and current hardware usage statistics for hardware such as memory, CPU, your network card, and your computers hard drive.

- Do not panic if you see a spike in usage that lasts for only a few seconds, short spikes are very common. However, if spikes are consistent and usually last longer than 10 seconds, that is an indication that there is something wrong.

# Think First Before Throwing Out That Old System

**I** would not be too quick to throw out the old computer; you may find good use for it. Perhaps you can donate it to charity, use it as a backup system, or find some other use for it.

> Before donating your computer, make sure that you properly delete the contents of your hard drive. When you delete a file, it is possible for someone to use special recovery software to recover it. So make sure that you use a utility that permanently deletes files. You do not want to provide software or your personal information to someone else by mistake.

- You can find free utilities on the Internet designed to permanently delete files. Some of these utilities can be put onto a floppy disk, allowing you to boot your computer using the floppy disk and run a program that permanently deletes all of your computers contents. Just do a simple Google search using your favorite Internet search browser for *"secure hard drive cleaning utilities"*. Read the programs instructions. I use a simple program called *Darik's Boot and Nuke*.

## You Cannot Just Copy Programs From One Computer To Another:

This is important to remember. You cannot just copy the directory contents of a program from one computer to another and expect it to work. Even if this does work for a particular program, the program may not operate properly.

> For programs to work correctly, they need to be able to configure themselves to work on the particular computer system that you are installing it on. This normally only happens when you click on the setup icon during the initial program installation.

> Never throw away your program disks, you never know when you will need them again. Sometimes program disks are required when you are installing new hardware, or making other modifications to your computer.

- On a *Windows* based computer, unless you have multiple users with their own user accounts, you only need to click on the program installation icon to start the installation process, otherwise you should use the *Add/Remove Programs* feature in the control panel to install programs. During the installation, you may be asked a few questions, but that is generally the extent of it.

- For other operating system types, such as *UNIX* and *Linux*, you generally run a special command line script or you install the program using the operating systems graphical program installation utility if it has one.

## Other Uses for Your Turtle:

If you know a technician that can help you network your computers together, you could have them create a link between your computers to so that you can easily backup important files.

I have actually set up old computers with the *Linux* operating system and have turned them into firewalls, routers, storage servers, [17]DHCP servers, and even web servers, and they usually work excellent.

---

[17] A DHCP server is a special server that assigns your computer an Internet protocol address that allows your computer to connect to networks, including the Internet.

# Connecting To the Internet

Getting on the Internet is simple. If you live in an urban area, chances are you have an Internet Service Provider that can provide high-speed Internet access to you. High-speed cable or DSL Internet is available in most areas, including many rural areas. Dial-up Internet is available just about everywhere, but it is slow and prevents you from viewing some sites properly. If high speed Internet is available and you can afford the extra few more dollars per month, then it is worth considering over dial-up Internet.

- ➢ Your first step to getting on the Internet is to contact a local Internet Service Provider for your area. In many cases, this will be either your telephone or your cable service provider. They will be able to tell you if they offer services in your area. Just search the yellow pages or ask friends whom they would recommend for Internet services.

- ➢ When contacting an Internet service provider, it is helpful if you know the specifics of your computer, such as what operating system you are using, and how much RAM your computer has.

- ➢ Depending on your connection type and the services offered by your ISP (Internet Service Provider), either they will send a technician to your house to install your service for you, or they will send you a package for you to setup yourself.

- • Dial-up Internet connections block your telephone line. If you need your telephone line to be free while you surf the Internet, then go with a high-speed Internet connection.

- • DSL (Digital Subscriber Line) high speed Internet does use your telephone line, but it does not prevent you from using your telephone on a normal basis because the Internet connection itself uses a different frequency range than a regular voice telephone call, allowing you use your telephone line and the Internet at the same time.

For a simple dial-up Internet connection, all you need installed on your computer is a dial-up modem.

- • Dial-up Internet is a relatively old technology, and most new computers will not come with dial-up Internet connection hardware. If only dial-up Internet is available in your area then you have to have a dial-up modem installed in your computer if it does not already have one. You can easily identify one of these devices. They are located on the back of your computer (if it has one) (or on the side of your laptop) and have two telephone jacks (or one in the case of most laptops), one that connects to your telephone wall jack, and another one that connects to your telephone. Do not confuse these with Ethernet jacks, which have eight pins, but look very similar.

You also need a username, password, telephone number to dial in to, and possibly other settings that you will need to obtain from your Internet Service Provider.

- New computers come with a standard Ethernet port, which is slightly bigger telephone jack, although it looks almost identical. Remember that it has eight pins. This is what most home computers use for a high-speed Internet connection, no matter if you are using high-speed cable, or DSL.

➤ I highly recommend using an Internet service provider that has free 24-hour telephone support.

# Preventing Carpel Tunnel Syndrome & Other Injuries

Carpel Tunnel Syndrome occurs when certain nerves, which are located in the carpel tunnel of your wrist, begin to swell, creating a pressure in your hand. This is often the result of very repetitive motions, such as keyboarding.

Sometimes this can be painful, other times it may cause tingling or numbness in your fingers, hands, and possibly your wrist. Either way it is a nuisance.

If you do lot of sitting and keyboarding, make sure that you take breaks periodically and stretch your hands, fingers, and your legs to prevent pressure ulcers among other problems. In addition, you should purchase a wrist rest, which is relatively inexpensive. Proper posture also helps.

> ➤ I like the *Belkin* wrist rests that Staples sell, they are nice and soft and have a good feel.

Injuries such as back injuries and pressure ulcers can occur from an improper posture and sitting for prolonged periods.

Table chairs are not good long-term seating arrangements. Use a chair with a relatively high backrest that at least extends to your shoulder blades.

# Printer Paper

Ok, you are probably asking yourself; why on god's green earth is this person talking about printer paper. Well, it is actually quite important, because what you are printing should dictate what type of paper you are going to use.

- ➤ You need to consider the color, brightness, and weight of the paper, especially for printing important documents.

- ➤ Important documents should be printed on bright thick white paper. The brighter the paper, the sharper your document will look. I would recommend using white laser printer paper with a brightness level of at least 98 and that has a weight rating of at least 24 pounds.

- ➤ If you are going to be printing items with images, such as business cards and photos, then you will want to consider using glossy paper. The glossier the paper, the sharper and shinier the image will be. In this case, you should use paper with a weight rating of no less than 80 pounds.

- ➤ The thicker the paper, the less likely it is to curl, and the better your printout will be.

For general-purpose printing, any type of multi-use paper should work. Of course, you should save the most expensive paper for the more important printouts.

# Shopping for Software, Hardware, & Services

First, I want to apologize for perhaps being a little repetitive, but it is my job to help you, and I will. Here are some points for you to consider when you are shopping for items or looking for service. You can use these rules for just about any type of shopping experience, even non-computer shopping experiences.

## Identifying the Bad Stores:

(1) **Does it take more than ten minutes to find a salesperson to help you?** If so, perhaps the store is busy and does not have enough staff. This might be a one-time thing, or it might be an indication that the store has no interest in quality or customer service, too cheap to hire more staff, or maybe they just do not care about the customer.

(2) **Do the salespeople appear to have no interest in serving you?** If not then this could indicate that they have little product knowledge or they have a poor attitude.

(3) **Does the sales person appear pushy?** Are they on you like bees on honey the second that you walk through the door? This is a telltale sign that they may try to sell you what you do not need and make guarantees they cannot make just to make a dollar. A pushy salesperson could also be an indication that you are bothering them, and they want to get rid of you as fast as possible.

(4) **Does the salesperson seem knowledgeable?** While it is impossible to know everything about everything in the information technology industry, or in many other industries, a knowledgeable technician or salesperson should be able to answer at least half of your questions, and get you the answers quickly if they are unable to answer your questions.

(5) **Do the salespeople have a professional look and demeanor?** If the store plans to stay in business then they need to set standards and hire people who are knowledgeable, care about their appearance, and have a good attitude. If they allow an employee to wear jeans that hang down to their knees with holes, then chances are that you are not going to get quality service or products.

(6) **Does the salesperson have a know-it-all attitude?** People like this often do not know what they are talking about even when they think that they do. They may end up giving you bad advice. These types of people will say, "Hey, I

don't need any special training in this area because I already know what I am doing". If you get the sense that you are dealing with this type of person, then look elsewhere.

(7)     **What kind of reputation does the store have?** Have they been around for a few years? Are they some unreliable place that has just opened up? Stay away from the unreliable places when purchasing expensive items. If they have a web site, check it out and see if you can get any hints about their credentials.

(8)     **Is the store a size of a postage stamp?** Do not expect good service and quality from a store that is the size of a postage stamp and very cramped. This is an indication that the storeowners may be too cheap to spend money on anything of quality, a store large enough to move around in, quality products, and good service. I am not saying that all small stores are bad, but just be careful.

(9)     **Have you ever heard of the store illegally installing any type of operating system or software?** If so, then stay away from them, unless you do not mind having your computer electronically shut down on you all together, or much worse, paying a huge fine and spending a few years in prison.

(10)    **What sort of payment options does the store have?** Do you have the option to pay how you want? Is it a cash only store? While it is perfectly normal for an on-site technician not to carry around a debit or credit card machine, a reputable store or should allow you to pay by cash, credit card, or debit card.

(11)    **Are there any missing or damaged components?** Look for the obvious sings of damage, missing components, dents, bends, and odd-looking configurations. Do not purchase these components.

(12)    **Do you have a bad gut feeling?** If so, then leave and look elsewhere. Remember that you have a bad gut feeling for a reason, and more often then not, your gut feeling is right. If needed, consult with a trustworthy independent technician.

(13)    **Does the store have good warranty and return policies?** If they have bad policies then they obviously do not have a lot of confidence in the products they are selling. Keep in mind that you should not expect good warranty and return policies on used products. Check out my section on *warranties and return policies*.

(14)    **Do you find that you consistently have to replace damaged or worn products purchased from the same store?** If so, try purchasing your products from another store. Some products naturally have to be replaced over

time, such as printer cartridges. You should not have to replace your motherboard, hard drive, memory, processor, and similar items every year.

Sometimes brand name products are involved in some type of accident, so the distributors and manufacturers may sell these items to computer stores for a very low price.

(15) **Does the offer seem too good to be true? Are they sold out of the product that you are looking for?** This may be the old "Bait & Switch" technique coming into play. Watch out for offers that include free software. This "Free Software" often comes with strings attached, such as 60 day limited trial. Sometimes computer stores will advertise that they have a particular computer on sale, but then tell you they are sold out of that product. The trick is to bait you into their store by advertising good deals and sell you something else that is more expensive.

As another example, computer stores may offer free hardware upgrades. However, when they upgrade the hardware, they may be upgrading it to a lower quality component. Of course they will not tell you this in any advertisement. Again, this is another prime example of baiting & switching.

(16) **What type of support comes with the product?** Look for free 24-hour telephone support first. Most quality brand name products will come with free telephone support, an on-line knowledgebase, an on-line chat forum, and email support. Not all support is necessarily available 24 hours a day. Try to stay away from products that do not offer a toll free telephone number.

I have actually seen cases where the only support available for some products was through email, and in other cases, no technical support was available period.

To find out what type of support is available, your best bet is check out the manufactures web site as it will probably contain more information than what you see on the retail box.

➢ Since most *Linux* operating system distributions are open source (meaning that it is free for use), do not expect to find a toll free support telephone number for *Linux* products. However, there are plenty of free email and online support resources available on the Internet.

## Identifying the Bad Technicians

The following points apply both for in-store and on-site computer technicians.

(1) **What credentials does the technician have?** Technicians should have the $A+$ certification, be a *Microsoft* Certified Processional, and have a minimum two-year technical college diploma with at least two years of experience.

Some people may disagree. However, if they have proof of certification and a college diploma or university degree in information technology, then at least you know they have some training.

➤ Remember, your data may be more valuable than the computer itself. With this in mind, you should choose service technicians that have good credentials. You do not want to risk losing your data by having unqualified people servicing your computer equipment.

(2) **How much experience does the technician have?** Everybody has his or her own opinion, but personally, I would look for at least two years of experience.

(3) **Does the technician give you advice during or after servicing?** The technician may not give you all of the tricks of the trade, but they should offer good advice about things, such as what programs not to install on your computer, what technologies to look out for, and how to backup your data.

(4) **Do you find that you consistently require servicing for your computer multiple times per year?** This could be purely co-incidental, but if I were you, I would be suspicious if your computer is less than 3 years old and you require part replacement or other servicing more than three times per year. The technician could be poorly trained, or they could be intentionally performing other activities on your computer system that would force you to get more servicing done.

Use your gut feeling, talk to your friends to see whom they use for technical services (and find out how often they require servicing) and try another service technician next time if things do not seem right.

Of course, computers do breakdown as they get older, and some components, such as printer cartridges, regularly need replacement.

**(5)**     **Are you able to get a receipt when you pay?** Ask this right up front. This should not be a problem for you if you are taking your computer to the shop, or if the technician is coming to you. If you cannot obtain a receipt right away after you pay for services, then they may not be running a legit business.

**(6)**     **Does the technician have a business or tax number?** Keep in mind that this may not be applicable in some states or countries. In some provinces in Canada, it is a requirement if a businesses income is above a certain amount; you may want to check your local laws regarding this issue. If the business does not have a business or tax number, then they may not be a legit business, or perhaps the business income may be very low, indicating that they may not have a lot of experience. Consider looking for other alternatives.

**(7)**     **Does the technician present himself or herself well?** Do you want someone working on your computer who has holes in their jeans and has not washed themselves lately? Do you want someone who is arrogant and thinks they know everything?

**(8)**     **Is the technician recommending that you un-install your antivirus software?** Sometimes troubleshooting requires temporarily uninstalling antivirus programs. Some antivirus programs are known to cause problems with some computers. However, do not let the computer technician leave you with no virus protection.

**(9)**     **Is the technician offering to install software for you?** If so, then make sure what they are doing is legal. Your computer system can be electronically shut down, or you could end up having legal issues. A smart technician will realize that they too can get into the same trouble.

Also, they may be installing free, but poor quality software that may end up giving you more problems down the road. Do not let them install unknown rogue software.

➢ Beware of free antivirus products, they are not usually as functional as many paid versions.

**(10)**     **What payment options are available?** With an on-site technician, it is not normal to have the debit or credit card payment options, but if they do then that is great. However, you should have these options available if you are taking your computer to a shop for servicing.

**(11)** **Should I take it to the kid next door, or should I take it to a certified technician?** The answer to this question might seem somewhat obvious. If your car breaks down, you take it to a certified mechanic. If you have a medical emergency, you call the paramedics and see a doctor. If your water pipes break, you call a plumber. You call these specialists because they are specifically trained in their fields. Treat your computer with the same respect. Just because a kid next door may have made a couple repairs on a computer at one time, that does not mean they are a computer service expert.

❖ Someone once told me that because a particular anti-virus software package was well known, it should catch all viruses. How wrong he was. His mothers' computer had this particular package and it was infected by viruses.

➢ Ok, so maybe your computer is not worth $150,000. How much is the data on your computer worth? Things such as resumes, proposals, business files, and pictures are all important, so let properly trained technicians help you.

**(12)** **As always, go with your gut feeling.** If you do not have a good feeling about something or someone, take your business elsewhere. You are smart enough to read my book, so you are surely smart enough to trust your instincts.

## Now that you are considering making the purchase:

These are some of the most important things to be aware of, so I want to give you some quick, but good advice. Below, I talk about some of the most common components that people purchase for computers. Have a look at the following points:

**(1)** Carefully read the *"Warranty and Return Polices"* section in my book, I will give you some excellent tips.

**(2)** When purchasing computer hardware or software, have a look at the minimum hardware and software requirements before you make the purchase. Typically you will see minimum requirements such as:

❑ Operating systems supported
❑ Hard drive space required

- Minimum amount of RAM memory required
- Minimum processor speed required.
- Type of graphics adapter required.
- Minimum amount of graphic card memory required

➤ You may also see a section called "recommendations"; this means that if you have any hardware below what is recommended, the software may not perform as expected. It is important to differentiate between the requirements and recommendations.

• Please note that some hardware devices, such as processors, RAM memory modules, motherboards, and hard drives do not have specific operating system requirements.

**(3)** Make sure that the hardware or software that you purchase does come with operating or configuration instructions. The exception to this rule is RAM memory, which normally fits and installs into your system only one way.

**(4)** If you are purchasing RAM memory, make sure you get the kind designed to work with your computers motherboard. Be careful, just because RAM fits into the RAM slots on your motherboard does not mean that it was designed for your motherboard, and using the wrong type of RAM could damage your motherboard. For this and many other reasons, keep your computers documentation in a safe place.

**(5)** Make sure that any external hardware that you plan to purchase has the correct connectors to attach to your computer. If your computer hardware was manufactured after the year 2000 then it likely has USB connectivity support. Most external hardware devices have the option to use USB connectors if they do not already have them.

# Keeping a Cool Head

In the past, I have seen many people lose their cool due to technical problems. Losing your temper will not resolve your situation and can sometimes aggravate situations. About the only thing that you will accomplish is giving yourself health problems and having a hard time to find someone who will want to help you.

Computers are ultimately man made, and anything man made is never perfect. All computers break down at some point.

Computers are mechanical devices with software. Just like automobiles and electronic devices, at some point they will break down on you. The best preparation is to have a good backup scheme, which includes backing your data up to a different drive, and possibly having a backup computer system.

When comparing computers to other types of electronics, remember that computers have many more electronic components and a lot more software, both of which can become worn out or damaged over time., therefore, computers are more likely to break down over a period of time than any other type of electronic or electro-mechanical device.

By keeping a cool head, you will understand things a lot better because you will be able to think more clearly. Sometimes when I explain the reason for a particular problem to someone, they tell me that explanation does not make sense because their device or software did not have any problems the day before. Things always work the day before they stop functioning.

❖ I once was servicing a customer who understood computers very well. He was having technical issues and started getting angrier by the minute. He got so angry that when I asked him for the software CD provided by his Internet service provider, he did not understand what I was asking for. Remember, this customer had understood computers too.

## The best ways to keep a cool head:

➢ Prepare yourself mentally and understand that electronic things do break and that software sometimes becomes corrupted over time. After all, if everything were perfect then nobody would require computer and network service technicians.

➢ Prepare yourself physically and logically by having a good backup plan, such as backups of software installation files, data, files, emails, settings, favorites, and even a backup computer system if you can afford it. Also, keep paper backups of documents.

➢ Remember that the technician probably knows a few things about computers that you do not, after all, you are the one who is calling them for assistance.

➢ Realize that the technician may not be able to service you right away. After all, you are not likely to be the only customer that they have. Perhaps the technician also has another full time job or contract that they must attend to first. Perhaps they have higher priority issues that they have to resolve first.

➢ Remember that the customer cannot always be right in the field of information technology, simply because some things are not possible. Nobody can make a piece of hardware or software do something that it was never designed to do and expect it to work properly. For example, *Windows 98* was not designed to do some things that can be done with the *Windows XP* operating system.

➢ Ask yourself if you can still function in your day-to-day life if your computer or network or other electronic device were to break down". If not, then try to prepare yourself accordingly if something were to happen.

I have had people blow up at me before, and on some occasions, I have almost picked up my equipment and left. You should try to keep a good relationship with a technician or company if you want good prompt service.

• Getting upset is very normal, but if you are in a foul mood and are the type of person to snap at people, then perhaps you should just wait a day or so and cool down before attempting to have your computer serviced.

❖ I was once performing some service work for a customer. The customer wanted some programs copied from computer A to computer B because computer A was not working properly and it had to be re-formatted. I tried to explain why we could not copy programs from one computer to another and expect them to work. Finally, after an hour he grasped the concept. The reason why he did not initially understand this concept was that he was extremely irate, not at me, but the entire situation.

• If you are trying to solve a problem on your own and you find yourself getting frustrated, quit for a few hours and find something else to do. You may find that other ideas may come to you when you least expect it. This applies to simple computer troubleshooting and decision-making, or anything else that you may do in your daily life. However, I am not suggesting that you try to install complicated hardware and software, or that you make any system or setting changes on your own. If you are unsure about what you are doing, have a qualified technician assist you.

❖ When I was in college, I studied computer and web programming. As any programmer knows, one tiny error could cause your whole program to stop working. This would happen to me periodically and I would get frustrated after spending a few hours trying to determine the cause of the problem. I would start working on something else very different, and then in the back of my mind, something would click and then I would remember something or I would think of another idea that would solve my problem.

# Warranty and Return Policies

**S**ometimes people do not understand what they should be looking for in terms of warranties. Sometimes people think they know all of the questions to ask. Well, if you are either one of these types then you need to read this section closely. Read my points below; I will bet that you have not thought about some of the tips that I have to offer.

## Quick Tips:

➢ Always make sure that you ask about a store's return policy; in most stores, you will find that return policies differ between software and hardware. Specifically, if you buy a hardware component, you should find out at what point during the warranty you are required to deal with the manufacturer should something go wrong. Just because you have a 1-year warranty, does not mean you can return the item to the store should it cease to function.

➢ If you make a purchase from a chain store, check to see if you can return the item in a different country, state, province, or town. This is especially important if you are purchasing an expensive item and then moving to a new location shortly afterward.

➢ Keep your receipts in a safe location. Perhaps you could store them in a file folder, or in a locked cabinet somewhere. You will probably need them if you have to do a product return or exchange.

➢ Inquire if the business will give you a full or partial refund, or if they will allow you to exchange your item for something else of equal value.

➢ Ask if the item has to be un-opened if you need to return it. This is obviously going to be a problem if you purchase a product that requires you to open it before you can discover any potential problems. If this is the case, shop elsewhere. Most stores will not have such a policy for many items with the possible exception of computer software.

➢ Check to see if there are any fees for returning the item. After all, why should you have to pay because something is not working properly or was damaged before you purchased it? Some stores will charge you only if you return the product simply because you do not want it anymore, which is normal.

➤ Be wary of stores that ask for down deposits. In some places, there are no laws that say that you can get back your money if you change your mind about purchasing a product. In other places, laws say that there must be a written agreement for certain amounts deposited.

➤ For new printers and power supplies, you should be able to get at least a one-year warranty, while most other components should come with at least a two-year warranty, if not then be very careful about what you buy.

➤ You should also check whether the store that you purchase your items from would service or replace the items on the spot, or if they have to send the item back to the manufacturer for repair or replacement, which can sometimes take weeks. For some brand name computers, such as *Dell*, the company may send a technician directly to your site free of charge if your computer is still under warranty.

➤ Compare warranties between stores for the same item. If you can get a longer warranty for the same item at the same price at another location, then consider buying from the location that gives you the better warranty.

➤ Do not expect to get a warranty for used products. Count yourself lucky if someone is kind enough to give you a warranty in this case.


If you are not sure about what to expect for a good warranty for the product you are interested in, then ask a trusted and non-biased person for their assistance, or do an Internet search on products similar to what you are interested in and see what their warranty plans consist of. If you ask the commissioned salesperson in the store, obviously, they will tell you that their warranty is standard.

# Some Things You Need To Know Before Requesting Servicing

It is never a bad idea to get price quotes, but it may not be possible to get immediate accurate quotes depending on the problems that you are having with your computer, or depending on the type of service that you are looking for.

> ➤ Remember, without the technician being able to see your computer or your network, it is not always possible to diagnose all problems. Just imagine a doctor trying to diagnose an illness that a patient may have while simply talking to them on the telephone and not ever seeing them, it does not work well very often.

On the other hand, if your computer is in good working condition and you just want some software or hardware installed, such as a printer or scanner, then it is fair to be charged a set amount. For my business, I guarantee hardware and software other than operating system and server software to be installed within one half hour, and if it takes less time then I perform other services for the customer. If services take less than one hour, I perform other services for the customer since I do have a minimum one-hour charge for on-site visits.

> ➤ Also, remember that cheaper technicians are not always a better bang for the buck. Perhaps they are cheaper because they are new to the industry and do not have the proper skills, tools, and qualifications.

It is common for qualified technicians to charge between $40 and $100 per hour depending on the exact service that is being provided. This does not mean that the technician that charges $100 per hour is necessarily more qualified. However, if a technician charges an unusually low price, then they are probably not qualified, have little experience, or they have little intention of staying in business for a long time. Remember that the prices that I have indicated here are in Canadian currency, and are not written in stone, they are current standards as of the writing of this book.

## Preparing For Servicing:

Preparing for servicing is very important because it saves you a lot of time, money, headaches, and possibly your sanity too. Depending on the issue at hand, you may be

68

paying the technician or company by the hour, so take what I have to say very seriously. You should prepare both physically and mentally.

➤ As you always should anyway, make sure that you backup all of your important files, installation programs, disks that you get with your computer or associated hardware, and any important emails. If you are unable to do this, a good technician will be able to help you with backing up your important files and emails, provided that your computers hard drive is not malfunctioning.

➤ I know I have said this before, but I will say it again; never expect a technician to do an illegal installation of software. There can be huge legal consequences for both of you. You can be caught electronically. Even if no legal action is taken against you, there may be an electronic means of shutting down your computer system. Penalties for illegal software installations can exceed $25,000.00 USD and can include time in prison.

➤ With point number two in mind, make sure that you have all of your disks ready, including your operating system disk, regardless of whether you are taking your computer to a shop to get serviced, or if the technician is coming to your location.

➤ Do not be afraid to ask the technician for proof of their qualifications. A qualified technician should have the *A+* certification, *Microsoft* Certification, and a technical diploma with at least two years of training. Some people will say that you do not need to be certified to fix a computer, but through training, the technician also learns from the experiences and knowledge of teachers who have worked in the field for many years, unlike the uncertified person.

➤ Set aside plenty of time for the technician to do their job; not all issues can be solved in half an hour. I have had cases where customers would request my service at a set date and time at their home and then one half hour after I arrive they tell me that I should finish up quickly because they needed to leave to go to an appointment. Needless to say, the job did not always get finished.

➤ Before purchasing products that you are unfamiliar with, speak to a trusted qualified non-biased person who is knowledgeable about that particular product, such as a computer technician, before making the purchase. I have seen cases where people have purchased products that turned out to be useless to them.

➤ If a technician is coming to your location to install hardware, try to take the hardware out of any boxes ahead of time if it is large. Keep your hardware and software organized and readably available for setup, this may save you time and money. Keep your manuals handy as well.

➤ Make a note of any appointments that you have with your computer technician; you do not want to forget about appointments, this can be costly, and you would want to keep a good relationship with a good technician as well.

➤ Expect minimum charges for services, especially if a technician must travel to your site. Technicians and businesses who travel to customers sites take into consideration the amount of travel time. It is common for technicians to charge for at least one hour of servicing.

➤ Save your software disks, you never know when you might need them again.

❖ I once encountered someone who threw out a printer software disk that contained the software and drivers needed to operate the printer. I had to download the entire software package from the manufacturer's web site, which took about 2 hours.

➤ Sit back and let the technician do the work. However, be near by in case the need your assistance or have any questions. I have seen cases where I would open up a computer and then all of a sudden the customers would stick their hands inside and take wires apart. Most technicians, including me, will not be responsible for any damage that you do.

➤ Do not try to be the know-it-all type of person. In the I.T. industry, many things do not make sense to ordinary computer users. If something does not make sense to you, do not be afraid to ask questions.

❖ This is a true story. A potential customer once called me and told me they purchased some software and hardware that would allow them to copy installed programs from one computer to another, but they were not having any luck getting this setup to work properly. The truth is that these things may work for individual files and some program settings, but they rarely work properly for entire program installations. Some salesperson told them it would work just so they could make a sale.

➤ Large businesses typically purchase groups of identical computers. This can allow them to use a program that takes a snapshot image of a computers hard drive contents. Then they can store the image on a server for transmission to identical computers, or they make duplicate copies of the computers hard drive contents. You need to use computers with identical hardware configurations (CPU, motherboard, and hard drive) along with imaging software for this to work.

# Security Sense

In the past, some customers have asked if I can guarantee that their systems are completely secure. My answer to that question is always the same and always truthful, there is no 100% guarantee of security unless you disconnect your computer from the Internet or any network, unplug the electricity, and never turn on your computer. While this may sound grim, you can provide yourself with a reasonable level of security.

## Good Security Guidelines:

> Install quality well known anti-virus software on your computers and update the software immediately. Antivirus products are never up to date when you purchase them from the store as new viruses come out on a daily basis. Configure your product so that it automatically updates, runs a full system scan, runs in the background, and so that it automatically scans your email messages.

> Install at least two spy-ware removal utilities on your computer and update them immediately. Some well-known spy-ware removal software programs are *PCTool's Spyware Doctor (www.pctools.com), Spybot Search & Destroy, AVG's spyware removal untility, and Lavasoft's Ad-aware (www.lavasoft.com)*. You should run full system scans manually at least one time per week or more depending on your usage.

> Update and run your spy-ware scanners before doing on-line banking or purchasing as spy-ware can record your keystrokes and send them to a remote server without you knowing.

> Refrain from installing rogue programs on your computer. Such programs are not always tested properly for stability, and may contain spy-ware.

> Stay away from peer-to-peer file sharing programs as you may be connecting to virus and spy-ware infected computers.
> Stay away from on-line gambling and pornography sites. They often contain spy-ware and viruses that can steal credit card and other personal information from you, and damage your computer.

> If you are using *Linux, Windows 2000, Windows XP*, or a later version of *Windows*, configure your computer to require users to enter a username and password for security. In the case of *Windows* computers with *Windows 2000* and later, you can configure your computer so that users have to press the *CRTL +*

*ALT + DELETE* keys at the same time to log on to the computer. This helps reverse the effects of some password key logging software that may be on your computer.

➤ Install firewall software on your computer and configure it to protect your computer. If you connect to a home computer network through a router, the router will likely already have a firewall integrated inside it, make sure that it is configured so that only the required services are running and the required ports are open. If you are unsure how to configure a firewall then you should contact the device manufacturer or a computer technician. If possible, look for the necessary configuration information on the manufacturer's web site first. Go with a well-known manufacturer such as Dlink, Linksys, or Netgear so that you can get a good level of technical support.

• Some well-known security products can cause problems when you try to network computers together for the purpose of file and resource sharing.

➤ Never provide any of your usernames, passwords, personal information, or bank account information to someone or some website that you do not know. Read my section on Phishing Attacks.

➤ Update your operating system and software as per the vendor's instructions on a regular basis.

➤ Refrain from purchasing a wireless network if you do not absolutely need one. They are very un-secure by nature. Even though some level of security can be added to wireless networks, hackers have half the battle won because they have access to the transmission medium, which is the airwave signal generated by your wireless access device.

➤ Last but certainly never least, if you are unsure about what products to buy, talk to an independent professional.

## Spy-ware, Ad-ware, Browser Hi-jack Software, and Mal-ware

Spy-ware is typically used to obtain information off your computer and send it to a third party computer somewhere without you knowing about it. It comes in many forms and usually gets onto a computer by simply visiting a web site, or it may come integrated with a piece of software, particularly non-reputable free software that you download from the Internet. Free software is not always necessarily free. Just think what might happen if a key-logging spy-ware program recorded your credit card or banking information and then forwarded it to someone else without you knowing.

Of course viruses are considered forms of mal-ware because they can damage your computer. However, some forms of mal-ware are not detected by anti-virus programs and simply take up some of your computers resources.

> I have seen programs that actually take up some victim computers network bandwidth and give it to other remote computers, which of course slowed down the affected computer's Internet connection. In other cases, memory and processing power may be stolen from a computer for a remote computer to use.

> Ad-ware, as the name suggests, is used to send advertisements to your computer. This can be quite an annoyance, and not to mention a security risk if you purchase products from these advertisements.

> Browser hi-jack software configures the settings of your Internet web site browser to re-direct your browser to different or fake web sites. This becomes a nuisance and a security risk if you often have to input personal information such as a username and password to access a web service, or if you do on-line banking transactions. Use multiple well-known spy-ware removal utilities to remove these threats.

> Do not ever respond to any email messages or pop-ups telling you that your computer is infected and that you need to download or purchase software to remove the infections. These messages will only guide you to more mal-ware. After all, a thief would not break into a bank and then call the police on themselves.

> Refrain from using your computers administrator account as much as possible. Create a standard user account. Many spy-ware programs get onto your computer based on the privileges of the account that you are currently using. If you are logged on using an account that does not have the rights to install programs, then most spy-ware programs cannot install themselves on your computer.

## Phishing Attacks:

Never under any circumstances should you ever respond to any emails asking you for personal information, no matter who sends the email.

> You may get emails by persons pretending to be representatives of financial institutions saying that your accounts have been locked, and to unlock them you

need visit a web site and input information. If you follow their instructions then you might as well just give a thief your bank card and pin number or other personal information, because that is what you are doing anyway.

I always receive these types of emails from people claiming to be representatives of RBC, CitiBank, PayPal, eBay, and all sorts of other businesses and I just delete them. Generally, financial institutions will not contact you by email; correspondence is usually through regular mail. If you have any questions or concerns about your accounts, then you should talk to your institution directly.

> Never click on any of the links provided in any suspicious emails, web sites could be spoofed very easily. When in doubt, always type in the companies web site address manually, or better yet, call the institution if you have any concerns.

If you want to see some examples if phishing emails, I have given you four of them on the following pages.

These emails are on a word-for-word basis typed exactly how it showed in my email. Take note of the spelling mistakes and incorrect grammar. For legal and professional reasons, I have left out actual company names.

**Phishing Example 1:**

Good afternoon, unfortunately some processings have been cracked by hackers, so a new secure code to protect your data has been introduced by &%$^%$.

You should check your card balance and in case of suspicious transactions immediately contact your card issuing bank.

If all transactions are alright, it doesn't mean the card is not lost and cannot be used. Probably, your card issuers have not updated information yet. That is why we strongly recommend you to visit our web-site and update your profile, otherwise we cannot guarantee stolen money repayment.

Thank you for your attention.

Click here and update your profile

**Phishing Example 2:**

It has come to our attention that your *%$@# billing information are out of date. This require you to update billing information as soon as possible. This billing update is also a new *%$)#% security statement which goes according to the established norms on the User Agreement to reduce the instance of fraud on our website.

Please update your records on or before **February 15, 2006**. A failure to update your records may result on a suspension of your account.

**To update your *%$# records click on the following link:**

If, after reviewing your account information, you seek further clarification regarding your account access, please contact %$#% by visiting the Help Center and clicking "Contact Us". This new security statement will helps us continue to offer %$#% as a secure and cost-effective service. We appreciate your cooperation and assistance.

Sincerely,

The *%)$# Team

**Phishing Example 3**

This one is kind of funny, considering I did not have an account at the time that it was sent to me.

As part of our security measures, we regularly screen activity in the *%$@$ system. We recently noticed the following issue on your account:

Recent account activity has made it necessary for us to collect additional verification information. Case ID Number: PP-071-363-   053

For your protection, we have limited access to your account until additional security measures can be completed. We apologize for   any inconvenience this may cause.


To review your account and some or all of the information that    &%$#@$ used to make its decision to limit your account access, please visit the Resolution Center. If, after reviewing your account information, you seek further clarification regarding your account access, please contact %$@#% by visiting the Help Center and clicking "Contact Us".We thank you for your prompt attention to this matter.
Please understand that this is a security measure intended to help protect you and your account. We apologize for any inconvenience.

If you are the rightful holder of the account you must click the link below and then complete all steps from the following page as we try to verify your identity.

  https://www.(%$@#$()@#$(%#@)$(#$

  Sincerely,


  !@#_)$#%$$@


**Phishing Example 4:**


Dear )%$@#*%$Bank user,

We are looking forward to your support and understanding and inform you about new *%$@#$(%® department system updrade performed by security management team in order to protect our clients from increased online fraud activity, unauthorized account access, illegal funds withdrawal and also to simplify some processes.

The new updated technologies guaranty convenience and safety of %$#%(*@® account usage. New services for your account will be effective immediately after an account confirmation process by a special system activation application.

To take an advantages of current updrade you should login your account by using @#$%$%^^%® Online application. For the purpose please follow the reference:

https://%T$%#$

Please note that changes in security system will be effective immediately after relogin.

Current message is created by our automatic dispatch system and could not be replyed. For the purpose of assistance, please use the "User Guide" reference of an original ^%^%#%^® website.

Sincerely yours,
^%#%^%® Security Management Team.

For a more comprehensive understanding of current and ongoing scams, visit the *Scambusters.org* web site at *www.scambusters.org*.

## Wireless Network Security:

Wireless networks by nature pose a security threat because they use devices that provide radio frequency signals for the network connection. All networks, whether wired or wireless, have a transmission medium. The transmission medium for a wired network is the cable connecting the network components together, and the transmission medium for a wireless network is the air that we all breathe. For a hacker, having access to the transmission medium is half of the battle. To hack a wireless network, all the hacker needs is a computer with a wireless network card and the right software, and then in a short time they could have access to your network. Hackers could access your computers, use your network connection, sniff your network for usernames, passwords, or other transmitted information using a [18]packet-sniffing program, or possibly hack into your wireless router.

❖ There are known cases where people have actually driven around with wireless enabled laptops and have successfully connected to wireless networks in order to perform illegal actions.

• Every computer and network that connects directly to the Internet has an Internet protocol address (*IP address*) which is unique. This information is stored and recorded on server computers throughout the Internet and can be traced back to your home network, or your computer. If someone is connected to your network and performing illegal actions, the police may come knocking on your door.

**If you decide to build a wireless network here are some tips that you should follow:**

➢ Do not leave your wireless devices turned on when they are not in use, namely your router. Your router is consistently broadcasting a network signal for wireless computers to connect to each time you turn it on.
➢ Change the default username and password on your router to something that you can easily remember but hard for others to guess. This goes for the username and password used to access the routers configuration utility, and for obtaining a network connection. You can read your routers instructions manual on how to do this, contact your routers technical support department, or have a qualified technician do this for you.

➢ Configure your wireless routers firewall if it has one. Again, your device's manual or technical support department should be able to explain to you how to configure this.

➢ Using the routers configuration utility, enter a name for your network. You should always change the default name that is assigned because it is too easy for hackers to guess if they are familiar with the basic settings of common routers. Look this up in your routers manual as well.

➢ Set encryption on both your router and wireless network card as recommended by the manufacturer of your router; usually you will use an encryption algorithm

---

[18] A packet sniffing program is a program used to inspect packets of data transmitted over a network. These programs are usually designed to test network quality, but can also look at the contents of data packets.

called *WEP (Wired Equivalent Privacy)* or *WPA (Wi-Fi Protected Access)* on both devices. You will want to use the highest encryption setting possible. Usually you will have to apply the same settings to your router and your network card, and a username and password for a network connection will have to be entered on the router and the wireless network card as well.

➢ Do not mix and match different brand names. You should use the same brand name for both your router and wireless network cards for better compatibility, security, and proper technical support. After all, if you only have to call one manufacturer for technical support, it would be much easier.

➢ Install and update both anti-virus and anti-spyware products on all of your computers.

➢ Install firewall software on your computers.

➢ Routinely install *Microsoft* or other operating system and software updates.

Although I have provided you with some good quality tips for building and maintaining a wireless network, I cannot make my guarantees at all in terms of security. No matter how much you secure your network, there is the possibility that a hacker could hack into it with time and the right programs that are available on the Internet.

# Backing Up Your Computer and Files

This is probably the most important topic that you will want to read, especially if the data on your computer is worth more than your computer.

The topic of backing up your computer is a very broad topic, but I will cover many of the most important items.

## Backing Up Your Files:

This is very important, but not many people do it. Just think about how you would feel if your computers hard drive quit working and you lost all of your business files, resumes, and other important documents.

> People used to back up their files to floppy disks, but files are becoming larger these days, so floppy disks are no longer a viable means of backing up files. In addition, floppy disks do not have a long shelf life.

Using a CD or DVD burner with a CD or DVD R/W (Rewritable) disk is a good option for backing up files. However, some burning programs erase the disks first then burn to it (if it is a rewritable disk). Get into the habit of storing all of your important files in a common folder on your computer, such as the "*My Documents*" folder on *Windows* based computers. Then when you want to backup your files, you simply burn (copy your files using the disk copying utility for your burner) the folder that you have chosen to store all of your important files over to the disk.

- The burning options that you will have depend on the options that your burning program has within it, the capabilities of the burner itself, the speed at which the disks will allow you to burn at, and the speed at which the disk and the burner will allow you to burn.

> Using a USB removable pen drive as a permanent backup solution is very risky. These devices are small and could easily get lost. However, they are great for temporary storage and transferring of files between computers.

➢ External USB hard drives are probably the best option. They are much bigger than a USB pen drive so they are not as susceptible to loss or misplacement due to their size. In addition, they have storage capacities similar to a computers internal hard drive, unlike USB pen drives, which are very limited in storage size. Unlike CD-R's you can write to them as many times as you want and you do not need a special program to operate these devices.

➢ While on the topic of USB devices, I quickly want to mention that you can plug these devices into your computer while it is turned on, but do not try this with any device that uses a different type of connection as you could damage your computer.

➢ If you are using a *Windows 2000* or later, or a current *Mac* operating system, your computer should recognize a USB device as soon as you plug it into your computer.

➢ Again, that old computer may also be able to be networked to your new machine and used as a backup device.

➢ Test your backup scheme before you need to restore your data. Make sure that you can restore your files correctly.

The recommended method for testing backup schemes is to create a test folder, backup the files that you want backed up, and then do a test session and restore the files in the test folder that you created. Do some research on the backup methods and technologies that your operating system uses. In the case of *Microsoft Windows*, it is a good idea to understand what the terms normal backup, copy, incremental backup, and differential backup mean.

➢ No matter what backup scheme you use, you must have at least one full backup copy of your files.

➢ A normal backup does a backup of everything that you have selected to be backed up, no matter if it has already been backed up and has not changed recently.

➢ An incremental backup plan requires one full backup. It then, on a daily basis, backs up only the files that have been added or changed in the directories that you have selected to back up and puts these backups into different files for each day. So lets say that you perform a full backup each Sunday, then incremental backups on Monday, Tuesday, Wednesday, and then on Thursday your hard drive fails, you would have to first restore the full backup file created on Sunday, then restore Monday's, Tuesday's, and Wednesday's incremental backup files. If you lose one of these files, you will lose data for that period.

➤ Differential backup schemes require only two backups to be created. You first need to do a full backup of the files that you have selected. After doing the full backup, you would then perform a differential backup. A differential backup backs up everything that has been added or changed in the directories that you have selected in your full backup since you last completed a full backup into one file instead of having separate files for each day.

➤ A copy will perform a full backup, but it is not considered a full backup by the incremental and differential backup schemes.

## Backup Power Supply/Un-interruptible Power Supply (UPS):

Backup power supplies help save your computer and files from loss or damage during a power failure. Sudden shutdowns of your computer have negative consequences. You can lose data, or the capability to use your computer if you experience a sudden shut down.

Home backup UPS devices have a battery that turns on when the power goes out. This switchover of power happens so rapidly that your computer does not notice it. These devices come with software and a cable connection that allows you to connect your computer to the device to monitor its status. You can normally configure the UPS device software to save your work and shutdown your computer at a certain interval when the power goes out to preserve battery power and give your computer a proper shutdown.

For some of the more expensive UPS devices, your computer will run strictly off of the battery at all times. The battery in turn runs off A/C power to keep it constantly charged. The benefit of this is that your computer gets cleaner power.

High quality backup UPS devices will also emanate a sound when the power goes out. This option is normally configured through the monitoring software. If the computer is in your room, this will wake you up, which is not a bad feature if you have an important meeting the next morning and your alarm clock will not function without AC power.

UPS devices typically come with at least 4 to 6 outlets, and usually half of the outlets are connected to the battery. All outlets are usually surge protected.

- *APC* (*American Power Conversion*) and *Belkin* are the two major Backup UPS device manufacturers.

> ➤ It is important that you do not overload backup UPS devices. Printers, especially laser printers, may very well overload these devices and damage them. You generally should not run more than one computer (or a small server) and one monitor for each device.

> ➤ You need to look for the VA rating. The higher the rating, the longer your devices will run on battery standby. The VA rating represents voltage x amps. A 500VA rating is generally sufficient for one computer and a monitor, however, I personally prefer nothing less than a backup UPS with a 650VA rating for a bit more flexibility.

In most cases, you should not expect battery backups to operate on standby for more than a few minutes. If you are running a business server then you should dedicate one backup UPS to one server and purchase a device with a rating much higher than 650VA. Depending on the size, power consumption, and purpose of the server computer, you may want to purchase a UPS device with a 1000 or higher VA rating.

# Getting the Software

**O**k, so you have either decided that you are going to purchase a new computer, or software for your current computer, but you are new to this so you have no idea what you need or where to find it. I am going to give you some straight-to-the-point tips and hints.

The software that you choose to install should be only from a reputable source whether you pay for it, or if it is free. I accept no responsibility for any of the software that you install and any consequences that arise from installing the software. However, the software that I do recommend has been tried and tested and has withstood the test of time and has lots of documentation available.

## Operating System:

As I mentioned earlier, your computer will not operate without the operating system. All electronic devices have some sort of software operating system. The tips that I provide in this section apply more to non-free operating systems, such as those produced by *Microsoft*.

> ➤ If you install a free operating system such as *Linux*, do not expect the vendor to be liable for anything. Also, do not expect free support, although you can find it on the web. After all, you are getting it free.

> ➤ Confirm whether the product is an OEM or Retail version (unless it is free). Generally, the OEM versions are cheaper, but you are often more limited in the number of installations that you can perform.

> ➤ Do not bother purchasing "Upgrade Only" versions of any operating system or software; as the name suggests, they are not full versions and will not work if you do not already have a working operating system or working version of the software installed on your computer. These versions contain only the upgraded files, not all of the required files.

> ➤ If you plan to upgrade a piece of software or an entire operating system, make sure you can do the upgrade. Sometimes you cannot upgrade from one version to another. Take *Windows Vista* for example, you cannot upgrade from *Windows 2000* to *Vista*. However, you can do a parallel install, meaning that you can still have the choice of running both operating systems on your computer.

> ➤ When upgrading an operating system, especially a *Windows* based system, check to see if the operating system has an upgrade advisor program that you can download and install on your current operating system. These programs will check for conditions that prevent you from doing an upgrade or that may cause problems after you do an upgrade.

- *Microsoft Virtual PC* is a piece of software that allows you to run multiple operating systems on your computer by creating virtual computers on your system. You can download it free from download.microsoft.com. You can also install *Linux* and *Apple Macintosh* operating systems on *Microsoft Virtual PC* as well. However, there is quite a drawback in performance because you are essentially dividing your computers resources between all operating systems if you operate them at the same time.

## Email:

Email programs come as part of the *Microsoft*, *Macintosh*, and *Linux* operating systems, so there is no need to purchase such a program to be able to send email to your family or friends.

*Mozilla* (www.mozilla.org) makes a well-known email program called *Thunderbird*. It is an alternative to other standard email programs. If you do not like the email program that you are using, you can try another one. You can even try downloading free email client programs from the well-known download sites that I mention later on this section.

A fully functional email program should allow you to create mailing lists, folders, and mail filtering rules so that you can filter email to specific email folders based on the senders email address or the contents of the subject line in senders email.

## Text, presentation, and database software:

These programs typically come as part of an office suite. The most common office suite for *Microsoft Windows* is the *Microsoft Office Suite*. The cost for this will depend on the version that you choose. Some versions have more components than others do, but they usually all have the *Microsoft Word, Power Point, Excel, and Access* components. You can expect to pay a few hundred dollars for this office suite, but it has many good tools.

*Microsoft's* equivalent office suite (or almost) for *Linux* is the *Open Office Suite*, which actually has a version for *Macintosh* and *Microsoft* too, and it is free.

➢ There are a few differences between *Open Office* and *Microsoft Office*, such as available fonts. For this reason, you should use common fonts if you are going to be using a file between different programs, or continue to use the same version of the same program.

## Internet Browser Software:

Most operating systems come with Internet browsing software, so there is no need to purchase and install software for browsing the Internet. *Microsoft* comes with *Internet Explorer*, and *Linux* usually comes with *Netscape* or *Konqueror*.

If you do not like your current Internet browser, there are many more free browsers available on the Internet. You can download one from just about any free download site. *Mozilla's Firefox* is a popular alternative to *Microsoft's Internet Explorer*. It is highly recommended and used by a high percentage of computer users. You can also install *Netscape* for the *Windows* operating system as well.

I recommend that you install more than one browser program on your computer; if one fails, you have the other one to use.

## Anti-virus and Security Software:

There are many good solutions out there. You can purchase this software from any major computer component retailer. Some products have different capabilities than others. I know from experience that some solutions are better than others. Some products can slow down your system substantially.

- Be sure to check out my entire security section in this book.

If you are using the *Linux* operating system, there are many free antivirus utilities such as:

- AVG Anti-virus (free.grisoft.com)
- Clamav (www.clamav.net)
- And more !!!

*AVG Anti-virus* is also currently free for *Windows* as well, and it does not slow down your system nearly as much as some other products. If you are not sure what product to use, have someone help you based on your needs.

You will also want some spy-ware removal utilities as well. Like you should with all other hardware and software components, get something that is reputable. *AVG* has a decent spy-ware removal utility. *Spy-ware Doctor by PCTools* (www.pctools.com) usually does a good job, as does *Ad-aware*. You can find this software by using your web browser and searching on the *Google* web search engine. Remember, you also have to update this software on a regular basis as you do antivirus software.

You will probably want a firewall as well to help keep hackers out your computer. Firewall software can also be found for free on common download sites such as *www.download.com*. If you have *Windows XP* or *Vista*, then you already have firewall software. In addition, most versions of *Linux* have built-in firewall software as well. Additionally, if you have a home network and you connect to a router (no, not your ISP's router, or a switch, or a hub), then you also probably have a hardware based firewall. *Kerio Personal Firewall* and *Zone Alarm* are two commonly used free firewall software packages.


## CD & DVD Software:


Generally, this software comes free with the purchase of a computer DVD player. You can also find player software at some of the free download sites. Most computer stores would also carry DVD playing software for a relatively reasonable price. If you purchase a laptop or pre-built computer system already with a CD or DVD player, it likely has the required software on a disk, or you can probably download it from the manufacturers' web site.


- *Cyberlink* is known for producing DVD software.


## Music Software:


*Microsoft Windows* comes with *Windows Media Player*, which is a reasonable quality program for most users. There is *Winamp* too (www.winamp.com). With these programs, you can create play lists. With Winamp you can even have song cross fading.

For you *Macintosh* users, the *Mac* operating system also has lots of quality music software that has amazing sound quality.

If you want fancy software with many add-ons, then perhaps none of the above-mentioned programs will be sufficient. In this case, you may have to purchase a program from a computer store, such as *Staples, Futureshop*, or *Best Buy*. Make a note of what features you want and need, and check out the capabilities of these programs.

If you have an *Apple iPod* player, then you will want to download and install *ITunes* from *Apple's* web site (www.apple.com). Using *iTunes*, you can listen to samples and purchase individual songs for a small price, currently at $0.99 CAD.

## Burning Software:

No, I do not mean the software that you throw in the fire because you think that it sucks. I am talking about the software that allows you to copy files to disks and allows you to make copies of disks.

- The two most common burning programs are *Nero* and *Roxio*. Initially, I was never a big fan of *Roxio*, but I have to say that lately they have been producing some great software.

- *Linux* typically comes with its own built-in CD burning software. If your distribution does not have built-in burning software, then you can probably do some research on the Internet for commands that will allow you to burn CD's and DVD's.

## Where to Get Free or Trial Software:

- www.download.com
- www.tucows.com
- www.topdownloads.net
- www.shareware.com
- www.freewarefiles.com
- And more!!!!

# Troubleshooting & Who to Contact

**M**any times, there are problems that can be resolved without having to contact a service technician, or having to call technical support and wait on the phone. Let us talk about most of the common issues that users run into.

➤ Keep a logbook of hardware and software that you install and any other type of changes that you make at all, whether its hardware or software related. This helps you troubleshoot future problems. You never know, something that you think is innocent could become guilty as charged in the future.

### Internet Connectivity Problems:

• In all cases where you have to enter usernames and passwords, it never hurts to MAKE SURE YOU DO NOT HAVE YOUR CAPS LOCK KEY DEPRESSED.

❖ When I first subscribed to high-speed DSL Internet, I had run into an episode where I my username and password would not work when I tried to connect to the Internet. I got frustrated and called technical support. They asked me if I Caps Lock button was on. I had accidentally pressed this button and did not realize it.

• Start with the basics. Check your cable connections to make sure everything is tightly connected. Make sure that all Internet and network related devices, such as routers, modems, hubs, and switches are powered on.

• You should also check any firewall settings as they can prevent your computer from working properly on the Internet or in any type of computer network. For example, it may stop Internet related software from accessing the Internet if it is not configured. Your firewall can be in the form of software or hardware. If you use a router to connect multiple computers to the Internet, then you are using a hardware-based firewall that contains software settings. Normally you have to use your web browser to log into these devices to change the firewall settings. To check your settings, use the instruction manual that came with the router, or call the manufacturer if you require assistance.

If you are using a software-based firewall, you may periodically get messages saying that certain programs are trying to access the Internet. When this occurs, you can configure the firewall software accordingly to allow specific programs to access the Internet. Some programs that you will want to allow access to the Internet are programs such as email, your web browser, chat programs, and your Internet service providers' connection program if required.

> If you use a router to connect to the Internet, then you normally do not require Internet connection software to be installed on your computer. Normally you connect the router to your ISP (Internet Service Provider) modem, and then configure your router with credentials provided by your ISP. You then connect your computer to your router.

- Many typical hardware based firewalls, such as those included in routers, block all inbound connections to your computer (unless you open certain firewall ports to allow specific inbound connections without interaction), but allow all outbound connections by default, so regular users do not usually have to make any firewall configuration adjustments when they use hardware based firewalls.

Settings can differ from firewall to firewall, so I cannot give you a detailed explanation about how to check your settings here in this book. On a hardware-based firewall, such as a router, you may have to configure the port settings, although generally the default settings are sufficient for most users.

If you were running a web based server, then you would want to open some of the connections, or ports through your firewall that that protects the server. The ports that you will open will depend on what type of server you are running, and what ports the server is configured to operate on. Most web page servers have default port settings that can be changed. For example, the default port setting for a web page server is port 80. However, if you change the port configuration of the server to 3600 for example, you would want to close port 80 inbound on your firewall and open port 3600 instead.

- A port is a logical electronic line of communication over a physical connection. You can have thousands of communication ports on a single network cable.

- By default, mail programs use port 25 to send emails to other users, and port 110 to receive emails because most mail servers use the (P)ost (O)ffice (P)rotocol and the (S)imple (M)ail (T)ransport (P)rotocol settings.

*My Internet is not working:*

First, you need to determine whether or not the problem really is your Internet connection, or if it is only your program. Perhaps the program settings have been changed to something that does not work properly with your Internet connection. If you are having problems logging on to your Internet connection, or if you are having any problems connecting to any Internet program that requires a username and password, such as email or chat, CHECK THAT YOUR CAPS LOCK BUTTON IS NOT ON.

If you cannot surf the Internet and are using a DSL or Cable Internet connection:

**(1)**   Try using your email program to send and receive email.

**(2)**   Try other programs that you use over the Internet too, such as chat programs.

**(3)**   If other Internet programs do work then your Internet is working fine, you likely have a browser or firewall setting problem, call your Internet service provider or a computer technician to help you if needed.

**(4)**   If none of your Internet programs are working, shut down your computer, router (if you have one), and modem, check all of your network cables between your computer and ISP modem to make sure that everything is plugged in correctly.  Also, check the power connection to your modem and your router and make sure that all power switches are in the "on" position.

**(5)**   Remove the power cord from the modem, wait 2 minutes, then plug it back in.  Wait for all of the normal lights to stay solid.

**(6)**   If you have a router, remove the power cord from the router for approximately 30 seconds, then plug it back in.  If you do not have a router, you may proceed to step 7.

**(7)**   With all of your cables tightly connected in the proper locations, turn on your computer and try to connect to the Internet again.

**(8)**   If you still cannot connect to the Internet and you do have a router, try plugging your computer into a different port on the router, reboot your computer, and try to reconnect to the Internet. If you are still unsuccessful, bypass your router by connecting your computer directly to the modem, reboot your computer, and try to connect to the Internet again.

**(9)** If you are still unsuccessful with connecting to the Internet, contact your Internet Service Provider and advise them of the steps that you have tried in order to resolve your problem. If you can now connect to the Internet, then you have a problem with your router and will likely need to replace it.

## If your email program is not working and all of your other Internet related programs are working fine:

**(1)** Make a note of the error messages that you are getting and disable your antivirus and firewall software. Sometimes antivirus and firewall software can interfere with your email program. If this solves the problem, try un-installing and re-installing your antivirus and firewall software. Remember to re-configure your anti-virus and firewall software after re-installing the software.

**(2)** If the first step does not solve your problem, contact your Internet service provider and advise them of the steps that you have tried in order to resolve the problem.

## If you are using a dial-up Internet connection:

**(1)** Check to make sure that the telephone lines are properly connected to the modem on your computer. The modem should have an indicator telling you where to insert what wire. If you have both your telephone and wall jack connected to your modem, you will know it is connected properly when you hear a dial tone on your telephone.

**(2)** Do not forget to check the connection to the wall jack. Some phone line filters may interfere with dial-up Internet connections if they are not properly placed. Generally, you place the phone filter in between the telephone and the outlet that it will connect to unless specified otherwise by your Internet service provider.

(3)    If you do hear a dial tone but still cannot connect to the Internet, call your Internet service providers technical support group, preferably from a phone on another line if possible so that you can troubleshoot your connection and receive assistance from them at the same time.

***My email is not working, but I can surf the Internet and my other Internet programs are working:***

First, make note of any error messages that you receive when you try to send and receive email.

➤ You should never change any type of server or authentication settings in your email program unless you are told to do so by your Internet service provider. These settings are very specific to the email servers in which your email account(s) reside on.

If you made any changes to your email program, try undoing them. If this does not help, or if you did not make any changes and your program simply stopped working for no reason, then you should contact your Internet service provider's technical support group.

## Printing Problems:

The life span of printers is usually much less than that of most other computer hardware components. Depending on how serious the problem is and how expensive your printer is, it may be cheaper for you to purchase a new printer, unless the printer is still under warranty. With this in mind, I would like to talk about some of the common printing problems that users run into.

***My printer makes loud banging noises when I attempt to print something:***

This problem happens with ink-jet printers and is most often a serious mechanical problem. As a general user, the only thing that you can do in this case is unplug the printer and have a look inside to see if there are loose items that may have fallen inside, or if there is paper stuck inside the printer, and remove it.

➢ A qualified printer technician has to be specifically trained in printer repair services.

*My printouts have white lines:*

Again, this most often happens with ink-jet printers instead of laser printers. This is usually the result of clogged or misaligned print heads. To try to fix this problem, follow these steps:

**(1)** Your ink-jet printer should come with a software utility for aligning and cleaning the print heads. You may have to run this utility multiple times and it will require printing paper.

**(2)** If your problem is not resolved after running such utilities 5 times, you may have to replace the printer cartridges. Just use your printer software program or manual and follow the steps given to you

➢ If you do not use your ink-jet printer on a regular basis, your print cartridges will probably dry out, making them useless.

● As a rule-of-thumb, use your printer at least twice per week to reduce the chance of your printer cartridges drying out. Laser printers do not have this problem because they operate in a very different fashion and actually do not use liquid ink. Instead, they use a power-like toner, which cannot be used in an ink jet cartridge.

● If you find yourself constantly replacing cartridges due to drying out, it may be cheaper for you to purchase a laser printer.

*I have an ink-jet printer and my print quality is poor:*

**(1)** It may be time to replace your printer cartridges, but first, try using the printer cleaning utility software discussed earlier.

**(2)** Have you made any changes to any printer settings? If so, try undoing those changes.

**(3)** Also, check the printer property settings, and if you can, try adjusting the settings. To do this, you normally have to locate your printer icon, right click on it, and then select either printing preferences or properties. The options that you have will depend on the capabilities of your printer. In particular, look for quality control settings.

> ➢ Remember that if you set the settings to maximum quality you will use more ink.

**(4)** If none of the above work, then you will have to replace your printer cartridges.

➢ When purchasing an ink-jet cartridge, take note of the number of pages that it is rated for at low, medium, or high image quality.

➢ In addition, take note of the printer and the cartridge make and model number before purchasing a cartridge, whether or not it is an ink jet or laser printer cartridge. Not all models of cartridges will work in all printers.

*I have a laser printer and the print quality is poor:*

**(1)** As with the ink-jet printers, check the printer quality settings. To do this, you normally locate your printer icon, right click on it and then select either printing preferences or properties. You should be able to locate the quality control settings. The options you have will depend on the capabilities of your printer and your operating system

**(2)** If this does not help, try taking the cartridge out of your printer and shaking it; sometimes the toner ends up on one side of the toner chamber, effectively reducing the quality of the printout. You may also have to clean the cartridge by moving a certain button or brush located on the print cartridge or the cartridge drum, from side-to-side.

**(3)** If this does not work, you will have to replace the toner cartridge and possibly (but most often not) the printer cartridge drum. This process is usually very easy and is generally just a matter of removing protection tape from the cartridge and placing the printer cartridge inside of the drum with little force to ensure it is seated properly.

Replacing the drum is an easy process. Normally it comes out with the cartridge, and when replacing it you normally just need enough force to ensure that it is seated properly in place inside the printer.

If you are unsure of how to do any of this, check the documentation that came with your printer.

With some makes and models, the drum comes as part of the cartridge.

➤ Remember that if you set the settings to maximum quality you will use more printer toner per page, so I recommend doing this only for important documents and images only.

➤ Also, when purchasing a laser printer cartridge, take note of the number of pages that it is rated for at low, medium, or high image quality.

***The lights on my printer keep flashing on and off and I cannot print any documents:***

This can sometimes happen if you leave your printer sitting around and do not use it often. It can also be the sign of an empty cartridge, disconnected or damaged cable, jammed paper, or a printer that must be replaced.

**(1)** Make sure you have ink or toner in the cartridges (depending on whether or not it is an inkjet or laser printer).

**(2)** Check your cable connections to ensure they are tight and not damaged. If you come across a damaged or loose cable, repair or replace the cable, then reboot your computer and try printing the document again.

**(3)** Check to make sure that no paper is jammed; even the smallest piece of paper can cause problems.

**(4)** Again, check for any loose items that may have fallen inside the printer.

**(5)** Turn the power to your printer off and on again. If your printer has a built-in network card, try unplugging the printer for 30 seconds, then plug it back in and power it up. If your printer is connected to a print server, unplug both the printer and the print server for 30 seconds, restart the print server first then after 30 seconds restart the printer.

**(6)**     If needed, restart the print spooler service.

If none of these steps solves your problem, then you probably have serious problems and will have to have your printer serviced or replaced.

If you spend $1000 on a printer, then it will probably be cheaper to have it serviced rather than replaced, but if you only have spent $90 on a printer, it will be cheaper to replace the printer.

## Sound Related Problems:

### *My sound was working but for some reason it stopped:*

Have you checked your connections? Perhaps you moved something and a wire came loose. Perhaps your dog or cat has been playing with your wires.

**(1)**     Double-check the connections between each speaker and between the speaker system and the back of your computer and make sure everything is firmly connected.

**(2)**     Almost all speaker systems have some type of power connection that runs from the wall outlet to one of the speakers. Make sure that your speakers are firmly connected to your power source.

**(3)**     With low volume, start playing a music CD for testing purposes, and let it play until you have completed all of the steps here.

**(4)**     On one of the speakers, you should find a volume control and an on/off switch or dial. Make sure the power is turned on and that the volume is not turned all the way down.

**(5)**     On most *Microsoft* based systems, you should see an icon that looks like a speaker down in the right hand corner of your program task bar. Double click it and make sure that the mute option is not selected for any of the settings, and make sure that the volume controls in this program are not turned all the way down or disabled.

**(6)**     After you have completed steps (1) to (5), try rebooting your computer and then playing a sound.  On a *Windows* based computer you should hear a sound when the computer boots up, unless you specifically configured your computer not to play sounds on boot-up.

**(7)**     If you are still not getting any sound, you can try testing your speakers by using another pair of speakers or set of headphones.  If the test works this time then you have a problem with your speakers, if not then you likely have a problem with your sound card in your computer.

**(8)**     If you have completed steps all steps up to this point and your sound is not working, then should contact a computer repair technician regarding this problem.


## CD/DVD – ROM Related Problems:


*I can't get the CD/DVD out of my drive:*


This is usually a sign of a bad CD/DVD, so once you get it out, try it in a different computer, and if you still have problems with the CD/DVD then you should discard it.


➤ One exception to this rule occurs when you are using the *Linux* operating system.  Most often the CD will not eject when you press the eject button on the front of your CD/DVD player.  This is because *Linux* logically mounts the CD/DVD player when you start to use it.  You either have to right-click on the CD/DVD icon and select "eject", use the "umount" command with the proper switches (normally umount /dev/cdrom), or reboot the computer (but try the two previous methods first).


**(1)**     On a *Windows* based computer, try booting the computer into *Safe Mode* by consistently pressing the F8 button until you reach the Safe Mode options screen, and then select *boot into safe mode*. Then remove the disk.

**(2)**     On any computer running a non-*Windows* operating system, try simply rebooting the computer.   When the computer starts to reboot, immediately try to open the CD/DVD drive and remove the media. For *Linux* based computers, please see my bullet point above.

### *My CD/DVD Rom does not show up now when I boot my computer:*

Most often, this is a loose or damaged cable, or a hardware configuration problem.

**(1)** Did you have any new components installed inside of your computer recently? If so, the technician may have accidentally moved the cable that connects your device to the computer without realizing it, or removed it and forgot to put it back.

**(2)** Did you have a new hard drive or CD/DVD device installed? If so then perhaps the technician did not configure it correctly. Since hard drives and CD/DVD devices use the same cables and connectors, they each have to be configured using specific jumper settings on the device. If one device is not configured correctly, it can cause other similar devices not to show up properly.

**(3)** Do you have a computer virus? I hope that you have an antivirus program that is up-to-date. Remember to update these programs manually once you purchase one, and configure the program to perform automatic updates.

If viruses are not the problem, then seek the help of a computer technician. If the problem arose after having any computer hardware installed, then contact the technician who did the work, maybe they made a mistake, maybe they are dishonest, but it is unlikely that the problem is a coincidence.

### Display Problems:

### *Sometimes my monitor is blank:*

**(1)** Does your monitor go blank if your computer sits idle for a few minutes? If so, most likely you do not have a problem. This is commonly caused by screen saver settings or power settings. Try pressing a button on your keyboard or mouse and see if it turns on. If so, then you do not have any problems.

**(2)** If step one does not solve your problem, then shutdown your computer and check your cable connections and make sure that you have no bent pins and that all of the connections are tight.

**(3)** If step two does not solve your problem, try testing your computer using another known good monitor.

**(4)** If you use a keyboard-video-mouse switch, try connecting your computer directly to your monitor. Perhaps the switch does not work well for your particular hardware configuration.

**(5)** If your problem is not solved by this point, then you likely have a computer hardware problem and you should contact a computer repair technician.

## Computer Boot-up Problems:

*My computer makes a consistent clicking noise in a particular rhythm when I boot up the computer:*

Typically, this is an indication that your hard drive has quit working on you, or that it will quit any minute. Hopefully you have your important data, emails, and software backed up. If not, then you have probably just lost everything or are about to lose everything. Have a technician look at your computer, or take it back to the shop if it is still under warranty.

*My computer says "no operating system found" or "ntldr is missing or corrupt" or "xyz file is missing or corrupt":*

**(1)** Is there a floppy disk inside your floppy drive? If so, remove it and restart your computer.

**(2)** Has someone been working inside your computer lately? Maybe there is a loose cable and the technician did not double check their work before finishing. Have the technician double-check their work.

**(3)** You may have corrupted system start up files, which can be caused by viruses or improper shutting down of your computer. At this point, you should have a technician look at your computer.

➢ Make sure that you always shut down your computer as recommended by the operating system manufacturer. On *Microsoft* based computers, you generally press the start button icon with your mouse, and then from there you follow the steps to do a proper shut down.

➢ Remember to update your anti-virus program on a regular basis, preferably on a daily basis. I know I keep repeating myself, but you would be surprised how many people do not listen to my warning.

***I just recently installed a Windows service pack, and now my computer will not boot up properly:***

**(1)** This could be a serious problem. Try booting your computer into "safe mode" by pressing the "F8" key a few times during boot-up and selecting the "safe mode" option. From there see if you can uninstall the service pack by going into *Windows Control Panel* and then selecting *Add/Remove Programs* and then uninstalling the service pack files from here. This may solve your problem. If you are unsure how to do this, have a technician look at it for you.

**(2)** If uninstalling the service pack software does not solve your problem, have a technician look at it and try to backup any data. Unfortunately, you may have to re-format your computer and re-install all of your software.

➢ This problem may occur when you install the *Microsoft* operating system service pack by running the *Microsoft Windows Update* utility. I highly recommend that you instead download the "network install version" or "full install version" from the *Microsoft* web site and burn it to a CD, or better yet, order the service pack CD from *Microsoft*.

## <u>Operating System Installation Problems:</u>

*I just purchased a new operating system but it says that I do not have the system requirements to install it:*

Let me guess, you did not bother making sure that your computer met the system requirements before making the purchase. Unfortunately, many stores have a no-return policy when it comes to purchasing software.

> ➢ If you get such an error message, consider following its instructions. Perhaps you will get lucky and only have to do a minor upgrade to be able to install the new operating system.

> ➢ Some newer operating systems have utility programs that you can download and install on your current operating system to ensure that it meets software and hardware requirements for the operating system that you want to upgrade to before you purchase the operating system. This is especially true for current *Microsoft* operating systems *Windows XP* and *Vista*.

# Using Common Sense

**I** hope that you have read all of the other sections in this book. It will help you a lot. However, I have not covered some things yet.

## Try before it's time:

I sometimes cannot understand why people do not test things ahead of time, especially when their job is on the line, or if they are preparing for an important presentation.

❖ I was once called to a meeting to figure out why a screen projector would not work with a laptop. It was quite important that this be setup and working properly for presentation purposes, especially since the company's high-level management including the president and vice-president were in attendance. As it turns out, we could not get the devices to work together properly right on the spot in the middle of the meeting. If proper testing was done ahead of time, the problem could have been averted.

## Look before you buy:

Most stores have a "no return" policy when it comes to software. That means if you buy it, then you keep it regardless of whether or not your system meets the requirements to operate the software.

- First, you should take note of your computer system configuration, especially your CPU speed, amount of RAM memory, your operating system, available hard drive space, and the type and amount of memory on your video graphics card. Once you have this information, then go to the store or visit the stores online web site and look at the system requirements on the software package and do a comparison between similar types of software. If you missed anything in your notes that is indicated on the package, then check that as well before purchasing.

❖ I once installed an antivirus program for client of mine. The program came as part of a security package offered by his Internet service provider. Nowhere on their site did it show the program requirements. The program installed successfully, however, his system then became extremely slow. When we called the Internet service provider to notify them of this issue, we learned that the program required a 192 megabytes of RAM memory, however his computer system only had 128 megabytes of memory. Luckily, I was able to un-install this package and install another antivirus package.

## Do not leave it lying around:

I must admit, at my own personal computer I sometimes have things to eat and drink. However, one thing that I do not do is leave food sitting around my computer, especially with having a cat that likes to jump on my computer desk and go to sleep.

❖ My very first computer was a Tandy HX 1000. I bought this computer when I was just a young teenager. One night I decided to drink a glass of coke next to my computer. I spilled the coke over my keyboard and onto my computers motherboard. This glass of coke ended up costing me almost $400 dollars.

## Okay, so what's the problem?

I sometimes get amused when someone calls me and tells me that their Internet connection is not working. It is one thing if you accidentally have your <CAPS LOCK> button pressed and you are trying to enter your username and password, but it is something else when the problem is due to the simple fact that a cable is disconnected. After all, if your car stalls on the highway, would you not glance over at the fuel gauge? First, check for the obvious, such as the network cable connections, telephone line connections, electrical connections, and broken or disconnected cables and connectors.

❖ A customer once phoned into a help desk complaining that she could not log on to the network. After a half hour of trying to determine the problem, it was determined that she thought that she was connecting to a wireless network, when in fact her computer had no wireless network card and there was no wireless router either, and her network cable was unplugged for some strange reason.

# Where to Get Training

**T**here are many ways to get computer training depending on what you want to learn, how much money you can afford to spend, and what type of learner you are. Are you looking to become an I.T. professional, or are you just looking to learn about computers? Are you a hands-on learner, or are you a visual learner? Can you afford to take classes offered in your location? These are all questions that you need to ask yourself. Obtaining I.T. training should not be difficult in most cases.

If you are looking to become a technical expert, then you will want to receive technical training from a technical program at a college or university with high standards. If you just want to learn to use a computer, then you can take individual courses at most colleges or universities for specific computer technology areas. In most cases, these courses are offered at nighttime or on weekends. If you are a self-learner, then you can purchase computer books from a local bookstore. For learning *Microsoft* software, *Microsoft* offers an excellent suite of books that will guide you step-by-step on how to do things.

- ➤ If you plan on purchasing books, then you should go along with books that have tutorial sections. Great examples are books produced by Sybex or *Microsoft* for technical certification. In general, most I.T. certification books will have tutorials and practice tests to help you learn

# Keeping your Computer Running Smoothly

Thus far I have talked about things such as keeping your anti-virus and spy-ware programs up-to-date, and the dangers of installing rogue unknown programs. Now I want to talk about some of the not-so-obvious things.

**(1)** Do you always need the latest and greatest software? Remember that newer software often has higher system requirements. If you do not plan to use the extra capabilities of the new software, then do not waste your money and time upgrading it. More often than not, it will slow your system down to a certain degree. The extra functionality comes with a price.

**(2)** Use the latest file systems. For you *Windows* users, if your operating system allows you to use the *NTFS* file system, go for it. It has many performance and security enhancements over the old *FAT* file system. You can switch your *FAT* file system to *NTFS* without formatting your drive by opening a command prompt window and typing in the following command: **convert c: /fs:ntfs** (c: represents the c: drive, you simply replace the letter "c" with that of the drive that you wish to convert).

**(3)** For operating systems such as *Windows XP* or later, set your system restore point. This will allow you to restore your computer back to a certain point in time. Do this when your computer is working fine though; it does not make any sense to create a restore point when your system is not performing great. In addition, when you set the restore point, make sure you include the current date in the restore point name. Do this on a regular basis. Keep in mind that this will not fix all of your computer problems.

**(4)** Use any disk cleanup utility to remove clutter on your hard drive. Doing so will give you back some space and may remove temporary files that slow down your system. *Windows* has the disk cleanup utility. There is also a free utility called "*Dustbuster*" that works on *Windows* based systems which does a great job.

**(5)** Delete your temporary Internet files by locating the temporary files setting in your web page browser program. For *Windows* computers, you can do this through *Internet Explorer* by selecting the *Tools*, then the *Internet Options* menu choice, and delete the temporary Internet files. In addition, you should lower the storage space available for Internet files. Doing both will clear up space on your hard drive and also ensure that you get the most current web pages when you surf a regular site.

**(6)** Aside from backing up your files, try to ensure that you do not have unnecessary duplicates of files. Prime examples are music files. Perhaps the same music file is stored on your hard drive, but in different formats. For example, mysong.mp3 and mysong.wmf could be the same song in different formats. Do you really need them in different formats? If not, then delete what you do not need.

**(7)** Most operating systems, such as *Windows* and *Linux*, come with wizard programs to accomplish many tasks for you; use them. Such examples are the networking wizards for setting up networks and connecting to the Internet.

**(8)** Run the disk defragmenter utility that comes with your operating system on a regular basis. This helps improve performance by taking fragmented files and putting them together, requiring less hard drive reads to open a file. Review your operating system's documentation for the particular utility used by your operating system.

**(9)** Get into the habit of performing regular system maintenance.

# Frequently Asked Questions

**A**s a self-employed computer service technician, I am asked a fair amount of questions. I thought that I would help you by providing some questions and answers.

Question:     Could you please tell me exactly how much it would cost to have viruses removed from my computer?

Answer:       This depends on exactly how much damage the virus has done to your computer. If it is severe enough, running an antivirus scanner at this point may not help you. In this case, your only realistic option would be to start fresh by re-formatting your hard drive and re-installing you operating system, your software, and your hardware device drivers. This is going to take different amounts of time for different computers depending on the speed of the computer, what types of software they need installed, how much software has to be re-installed, and how many device drivers must be installed. In addition, it also takes time to re-configure your Internet connection.

- The amount that you will pay for servicing will usually depend on the factors mentioned above, and whether or not you take your computer to a shop, or if the technician has to come to your location. There is often a minimal charge for services. You can expect to pay more per hour to have a technician come on-site to cover for travel expenses and time.

Question:     Should I buy a brand name or a custom-built computer?

Answer:       It is what's inside the computer that counts. Will the brand name computer do what you want it to do? What software packages will come with the brand name computer and as opposed to the custom-built computer? What are the warranties? What make and type of hardware does the brand name computer use? Is there any room for upgrading the brand name system in terms of memory and the number of available PCI slots? If not then you might want to consider having your computer custom built.

Often times brand name computers use the same types and makes of hardware that custom built computers use.

Have a look at the following sections in this book: *Understanding the Basics before Buying, Shopping for Software, Hardware, & Services, and Warranties.* You will get some good ideas and tips.

Remember that brand name computer systems may sometimes be cheaper than custom-built systems, but cheaper is not necessarily always better.

On a personal note, I like to custom build my computers because I can put what exactly I want into the computer down to specific brand names.

Question:    Do you think that I should throw out my old computer and get a new one?

Answer:    Well, buying a new computer is never really a bad thing. Eventually you have to upgrade your hardware, software, and operating system at some point anyway. New computers will have a lot more support for software and hardware. If you think that you need to purchase a computer and you can afford it, I would say go for it. On the other hand, perhaps doing a hard drive or simple memory upgrade will solve your problems.

I would not be too quick to throw out the old computer; you may find a good use for it (but do not use old components in new computers though). Perhaps you can donate it to charity, or find some other use for it, such as a backup computer.

If you have a technician that can help you network your computers together, you could map a network drive from your new computer to your old computer and backup important files in the click of a button.

Question:    What Internet service should I go with?

Answer:    This depends on what your wants and needs are and how much you can afford to spend monthly on an Internet connection. These days you cannot really do much with a dial-up Internet connection. Some web sites will not work properly with a dial-up Internet connection. I would recommend either DSL or Cable Internet.

In most places, cable Internet is usually faster than high speed DSL, depending on how many people in your area use cable Internet connections.

Some Internet service providers will let you bundle some other services such as cable television, cell phone, and regular phone service so that you can save money on your monthly bills, however, this sometimes requires that you sign a contract of some sort, so do your homework if you are thinking about going this route. Specifically, you might want to find out what the penalties are for ending a contract early.

Question: Why do I not have to re-enter my information in a web browser form when I go to log onto a site? Is my information being stored somewhere it should not be?

Answer: The information is stored on your actual computer. Your browser keeps a history in cache memory of what you typed in for online forms and sites so that you do not have to re-enter the information. If this makes you nervous, go into your browsers settings and clear the cache and temporary files along with the cookies.

Question: Why do I constantly see this security certificate screen every time when I visit my banks web site? Am I being hacked?

Answer: The certificate will say either that the site is who they say they are, or that the site cannot be verified as a trusted site. If the site cannot be verified as a trusted site, then yes, someone could be trying to hack or steal information from you, otherwise the bank is telling you that they are who they say they are. Either way, read the details of the security certificate. If you have any concerns, contact the business or institution directly.

Question: Is it illegal to run a server for a home or non-business user?

Answer: Certainly not, but your Internet service provider may not like it. Some Internet service providers do not allow it, and will shut you down if they find you are running a server. If you plan to operate a server that is accessible to the Internet, check your Internet service provider's regulations.

Question: My business partner and I want to use Intuit QuickBooks and access the same files from remote locations, is this possible?

Answer: First, you would need to run some type of file sharing server so that you can share the files. Second, your Internet service provider may not like you operating a server. Third, your program may not allow users to work simultaneously on the same file at the same time (for the reason mentioned in the next few sentences). Finally, even if you are able to run a file server and your program will allow multiple users to access and write to a file simultaneously, you, your partner, or your computer are bound to run into confusing problems if you have too many hands on your files at the same time.

Question:    Why cant me and my friend both write to the same file?

Answer:    This could be for any number of reasons.  Perhaps security permissions on the file are not set properly, or perhaps you are both trying to access the file at the same moment.

For file integrity purposes, your program may not allow multiple users to access the same file at the same moment for the reasons discussed in the previous question regarding the two business people that want to access the same QuickBooks file.

Question:    How much do computers cost these days?

Answer:    This is loaded question.  The cost is going to be different for most people depending on what they want or need their computers to be able to do.  The more you need your computer for, the more hardware and software you are going to have to purchase.

# Legal Issues

## Software Piracy:

One of the more common legal issues that I want to talk about is software piracy. There are some important things that you need to know.

It may be tempting to install illegal software, but what many people do not know is that you can be caught electronically. Not only can you be fined, but you can also be sent to prison. Both the distributor and the customer may be criminally charged.

This is why I will not illegally provide software under any circumstances.

Not only is *Microsoft* cracking down on illegal software users, but other software vendors are also doing the same thing. This is understandable since some of these programs require hundreds of programmers that are highly knowledgeable in programming.

There are open source operating systems, such as *Linux*, which are free for installation. There are also free software packages, but which are sometimes more limited in capabilities than paid versions of the software.

Often times free software is only free in certain situations, but not in others. It is common to come across software that is free for home use, but not business related use. If you are operating a business, check the software documentation to make sure that you are not illegally using the software.

Usually you will get a software agreement notice when you try to install software. Read it carefully; it should answer most legal questions that you may have.

# See For Yourself

On the following pages, I have compiled a list of images of various computer components and peripherals. I have also provided short descriptions of each component.

Figure 1:

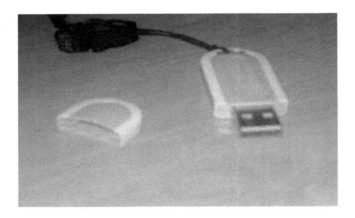

Figure 1 is known as a USB pen drive, or also known as a USB key. While these devices are great for temporarily backing data, you can see by their small size that they can be misplaced very easily, so it is not a good idea to use them as a permanent backup device.

Figure 2:

Figure 2 shows you an example of a computers power supply unit

Figure 3:

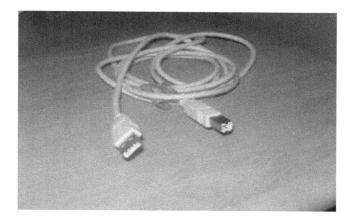

The image shown in figure 3 is a USB printer cable that can be identified by having one square end and one rectangular end.

Figure 4:

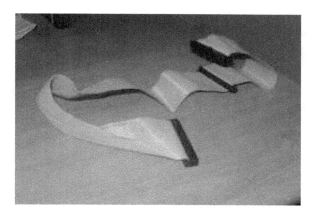

Shown above in figure 4 is an example of a 40-pin IDE hard drive cable. Some older SCSI devices use a similar looking cable with 50 or more pins.

Figure 5:

Above is an example of a USB hub device. It allows you connect multiple USB devices into one device to give you more capabilities.

Figure 6:

The device shown in figure 6 is a keyboard and mouse to USB adapter. It is great for adding mice and keyboards to laptop computers.

Figure 7:

Figure 7 is an example of an Ethernet network card. You cannot see it in this picture, but if you looked at one closely, you would see that the connector has eight pins.

Figure 8:

Figure 8 depicts a keyboard/Video/Mouse switch, otherwise known as a KVM switch. It allows you to connect more than one computer to a single keyboard, monitor, and mouse.

Figure 9:

Figures 9 and 10 show us an optical mouse.

Figure 10:

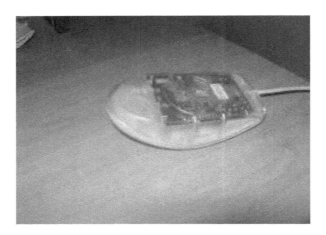

You can identify an optical mouse by looking for the red light at the bottom.

Figure 11:

Figure 11 shows us a cable modem. Remember that not all cable modems look alike.

Figure 12:

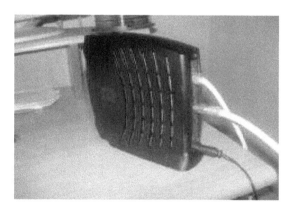

As shown in figure 12, cable modems are easily identified by the obvious cable connection in the back.

Figure 13:

Figure 13 depicts the back of a DSL modem. From top to bottom, you have the power button, telephone jack, Ethernet jack, and the power adapter connection.

Figure 14:

Here is the Ethernet cable shown in figure 14. It comes in all sorts of colors. It looks like telephone cable, but if you look at the connectors, you will see that they have eight pins instead of four.

Figure 15:

Figure 15 shows a sound card. Some sound cards may have more than 3 ports along with a joystick connector (the 15-pin connector that you see here). Generally, you have a green port for your speakers and other ports for input devices and surround sound.

Figure 16:

What you see in figure 16 is an Ethernet switch used to connect multiple computers together. Although they look similar to routers, they are quite different in terms of functionality.

Figure 17:

For you music lovers, figure 17 shows the iPod Shuffle. As shown in the picture, it has a mounting unit that allows it to connect to your computer so that you can add or delete music.

Figure 18:

Figure 18 shows us a *Belkin* wrist rest. It will help reduce your chances of developing Carpel Tunnel Syndrome.

To see an example of a computer motherboard, look at the next page.

Figure 19:

Here we have the motherboard in figure 19. Notice the extensive amount of upgrading room available. See if you can guess what the various sockets are for.

For the answers, look at the diagram on the next page

Figure 20:

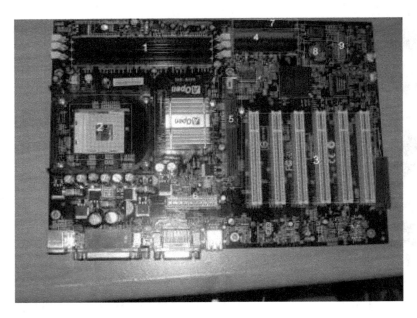

1. RAM memory slots
2. CPU Socket
3. PCI Slots
4. Hard Drive/CD/DVD IDE drive cable sockets
5. AGP video card socket
6. Motherboard electrical socket
7. Floppy drive socket
8. CMOS battery
9. Additional USB motherboard connectors for adding additional USB ports.

Figure 21:

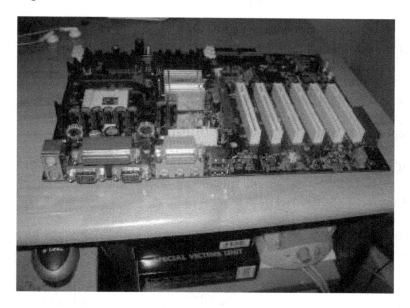

In figure 21, notice the integrated components on the motherboard. See if you can guess what each connection is for.

# Terminology

**AGP slot:**    This is a slot on your computers motherboard that is specially designed to hold AGP video cards.

**ATX:**    This is the name of a computer physical form factor design.  It refers to a computer casing, motherboard, and power supply.  An ATX designated motherboard or power supply will only properly fit in an ATX designated case.

**Bits:**    Refers to the size of an electronic data bus.  The bigger the bus, the better, because this means that more data can fit onto the bus at one time so more data can be transferred per each CPU cycle.  It also refers to portion of data.

**Cache Memory:**    (pronounced "cash" as in "give me the money baby") operates like main memory, but is much faster, and holds the most commonly used data for a much longer period.  It is generally built directly on to the CPU.  There are multiple levels of cache memory that are either attached to, or very close to the CPU, referred to is L1, L2, and now even L3.  Of the 3, L1 is usually attached to the CPU and is the fastest because it generally runs at the same speed of the CPU, while the other levels attach to the CPU by means of an electronic bus, which sometimes do run at the same speed as the CPU itself.  Obviously, the more cache the merrier, but you also have to consider the speed of the cache.  256K of cache running at the CPU speed will perform just as well as 512K cache running at half of the CPU speed.

Cache memory is also found on hard drives and video cards as well.

**Default Gateway:**    This is the bridge point that connects your computer to other networks.  It too has an IP address assigned to it.  An example would be a 5-port D-Link router.  A router has two types of network interfaces: internal and external. The internal network interface is manually assigned an internal IP address, and the external interface, which is the interface that connects directly to the Internet (in most cases anyway) usually gets its IP address automatically assigned by the ISP DHCP server so that the router can connect to the Internet on your behalf.  Also, store bought routers (not industrial devices) will usually have DHCP server built in that will assign your computer enough information to allow it to connect to a network.

**DNS:**    This stands for Domain Name System.  DNS servers maps domain names (such as www.google.ca) to the computers IP address where the websites actually reside.  This way, nobody has to know the IP address.  If you use a store bought router, it probably does have a built in DNS server.

**IP Address:**    This is a logical number that is assigned to your network card so that you can connect to the Internet or a computer network, and so that other computers can find your computer and communicate with it. This number is either assigned automatically by a DHCP server or manually assigned by a computer administrator. Without this number, you would not be able to connect to the Internet or other types of networks. When your computer connects to a network, if the IP address is not manually assigned, your network card should be configured to obtain the IP address, DNS server address, and default gateway address information automatically from your ISP or network DHCP server.

**Front Side Bus:**    This is an electronic connection on the motherboard that connects the central processing unit and the main memory together.

**Linux:**    Like *Microsoft Windows, Linux* is also a computer operating system. It is derived from the *UNIX* operating system, which has been around for a few decades. It operates much like *Microsoft Windows* and uses many of the same operation concepts. *Linux* also uses the same types of network and Internet technologies, so *Windows* and *Linux* computers can easily communicate with each other.

**Network card:**    This is a device that is either built into the computers motherboard, or is attached separately either by a PCI or USB connection and provides high-speed network and Internet connectivity capability to the computer.

**Packet Sniffing Program:**    This is a program that can examine packets of data, such as those that contain usernames and passwords.

**PCI slot:**    Stands for peripheral component interconnect slot. It is connected directly to your motherboard. It is used to connect expansion cards such as sound cards and network interface cards to your computer.

**Proprietary hardware:**    This is hardware that is non-standardized; it is designed to work only for specific computer or electronic systems, therefore it is not interchangeable.
**Recovery CD**:    This is a CD that comes with most brand name pre-built computer systems. It is used to re-install the operating system in addition to many applications and hardware device drivers. Please note that when you use the recovery CD, your operating system, software, and all files may be deleted from your computer, so you should backup your files on a daily basis.

**Server:**    A server is a computer on a network or the Internet that provides a function or service to other computers. Such examples are web pages and email service

**Optical mouse:**    Contrary to a trackball mouse, this mouse has a tiny camera at the bottom of it. It also has a red diode at the bottom of it so that light can bounce off a surface to provide light for a tiny camera. This camera takes thousands of pictures per second to detect movement and cannot be used as a standard camera.

**Parallel Port:**   This is a 25 pin female D shaped connector. It is used to connect non-USB devices such as printers and scanners. Chances are if you are buying new equipment, you will not need to use this port. Although the port is bigger and has more pins than USB, it is much slower.

**PCMCIA slot:**   This stands for Personal Computer Memory Card International Associations. This is used to allow additional devices to be connected to your computer. Such devices could be but are not limited to external network cards and CD/DVD drives. Generally, it is not found on standard desktop computers, but is usually found on most laptop computers.

**USB:**   This stands for Universal Serial Bus. It is a technology that allows you to connect devices to your computer without having to power down your computer. It also uses less system resources, and operates at a relatively high speed for good performance.

**Video card (Graphics card):**   This is a piece of hardware that provides you with all of your viewing capabilities. Either it is built into your computers motherboard, or it is a separate electronic card like device that fits into a special AGP slot on the motherboard.

# Credits

I wish to thank the following people for their much-appreciated assistance, which helped make this project become a reality:

*Jessica Carla Stovel*
*John Murray*
*P. Bruce Arthur*
*Pamela Biron*

Without their help, this project may not have become a reality.